What Others Are Saying

James Watkins tackles the big questions that most people ignore—or deny. I felt his heart in this book and thought, *I know those feelings*. I especially appreciate his writing about this and hope many will read this book.

Cec Murphey, best-selling author of *90 Minutes in Heaven*

This book is for everyone who's ever questioned God's goodness, love, or faithfulness.

With his trademark wit and wisdom, James Watkins addresses the hard questions, validates our pain, and offers a shoulder to cry on. This book shines a light on the blackest spaces of our lives and finds the hope that hides in the dark.

Renae Brumbaugh Green, author of *Morning Coffee with James*.

God, I Don't Understand is an amazing book that takes a fresh and intimate approach to the great "un's" of life. Through testimonies and biblical references, Watkins shows how to live in the light of God's love—despite tragedies, our lack of understanding, and resulting anger. They don't have to destroy our relationship with him.

DiAnn Mills, best-selling suspense novelist

You might not think that a book about unanswered prayers, unfulfilled promises, and unpunished evil would be engaging and encouraging. But it is. Like its author, this book is thoroughly honest, even gritty, but also helpful and hopeful. It is a pleasure to read and recommend.

Bob Hostetler, best-selling co-author of *Don't Check Your Brains at the Door*

I love the book! James pulls back the curtains of doubt and despair in the ancient psalms of Asaph. This book allows us to release our feelings to God without fear that our honesty might offend him. Take time to read through this honest adventure and find hope during seasons of struggle.

Chris Maxwell, author of
Underwater, his story of dealing with traumatic brain injury

James Watkins does a great job of making sense of many of the things that don't make sense to us. While being fully aware that God's ways are not our ways, I had many "aha" moments as I read his work. I'm sure you will, too.

Twila Belk, speaker and author of
Power to Be

James Watkins reminds us that we are not in danger of losing our faith simply because we have questions. So pull up a chair, settle in, and be blessed to know you are not alone. The road may be rocky, but hope and joy can be found along the way as God faithfully walks with us.

Diana L. Flegal, literary agent

Thanks to James Watkins for introducing me to Asaph, who reached down, stood by my side, and let me know I was not left alone to struggle with unanswered questions.

Louise Looney, author of
Over the Hill Onto the Mountain Top

God, I Don't Understand

Unanswered Prayer, Unpunished Evil, Unanswered Promises

James N. Watkins

God, I Don't Understand:

Unanswered Prayer, Unpunished Evil, Unanswered Promises

James N. Watkins

BVB

Bold Vision Books
PO Box 2011
Friendswood, Texas 77549

Copyright © 2019 James N. Watkins
Printed in the United States of America
ISBN: 978-1946708-41-0

Cover Design: Maddie Scott
Editor: Cynthia Ruchti

All rights reserved. No part of this publication may be reproduced, stored in a retrieval system, or transmitted in any form or by any means—electronic, mechanical, photocopy, recording, or any other—except for brief quotations in printed reviews, without the prior written permission of the publisher.

Published by
Bold Vision Books, PO Box 2011, Friendswood, Texas, 77549 USA
Originally published as *The Psalms of Asaph*
All Scripture quotations, unless otherwise indicated, are taken from the *New American Standard Bible*® (NASB), copyright © 1960, 1962, 1963, 1968, 1971, 1972, 1973, 1975, 1977, 1995 by The Lockman Foundation. Used by permission. www.Lockman.org.

Scripture quotations cited NLT are taken from the *Holy Bible, New Living Translation*, copyright © 1996, 2004, 2007, 2013 by Tyndale House Foundation. Used by permission of Tyndale House Publishers, Inc., Carol Stream, Illinois 60188. All rights reserved.

Scripture quotations marked (NIV) are taken from the Holy Bible, New International Version®, NIV®. Copyright © 1973, 1978, 1984, 2011 by Biblica, Inc.™ Used by permission of Zondervan. All rights reserved worldwide. www.zondervan.com The "NIV" and "New International Version" are trademarks registered in the United States Patent and Trademark Office by Biblica, Inc.™

Excerpts from *The Imitation of Christ: Classic Devotions in Today's Language* by author and published by Worthy Inspired, an imprint of Worthy Publishing Group, a division of Worthy Media, Inc. copyright © 2016.

Excerpts from *My Utmost for His Highest*® by Oswald Chambers, edited by James Reimann, © 1992 by Oswald Chambers Publications Assn., Ltd., and used by permission of Discovery House, Grand Rapids MI 49501. All rights reserved.

Excerpts from *Squeezing God Out of Bad* by author and published by Lighthouse Publishing of the Carolinas, copyright © 2013.

Names have been changed where individuals wished to remain anonymous.

Dedication

**To those struggling.
There is hope!**

Table of Contents

Acknowledgments	**11**
Introduction	**13**

Unanswered Prayer
1. Is Unanswered Prayer God's Fault? Part One	35
2. Is Unanswered Prayer God's Fault? Part Two	47
3. Is Unanswered Prayer Someone Else's Fault?	63
4. Is Unanswered Prayer My Fault?	73

Unfulfilled Promises
5. Are God's "Promises" Really Promises?	89
6. Are the Promises Conditional?	107
7. Are the Promises to Be Fulfilled in the Future?	111

Unpunished Evil
8. Is God Responsible for Evil?	127
9. Why Doesn't God Seem to Prevent Evil?	143
10. Why Is God Slow in Bringing Judgment?	151

Answers
11. Life is Hard	167
12. God is Good	177
13. There is a Purpose	185

About the Author	**211**
Endnotes	**212**

Acknowledgments

My wife and I always stay for movie credits, partly to reflect on the film and partly to acknowledge the hundreds of people from grips to gaffers to best boys who made it all possible. And, of course, there are often surprises at the very end.

So, I would like to roll the credits for all the wonderful people who made this book possible. A book is never a one-person production. Heartfelt thanks to:

Gloria Penwell-Holtzlander, first-reader, and George and Karen Porter, publishers, for believing in this project.

Beta readers who critiqued the rough first draft and kept it—and me—honest, authentic, and transparent: John Bray, Wenda Clement, Sandra Fischer, Diana Flegel, Renae Brumbaugh Green, Pat Holland, Lissa Halls Johnson, Cec Murphey, Andrea Arthur Owan, Cheryl Paden, Marilyn Turk, Bonnie Wheeler, and Joe Yates.

Lissa Halls Johnson and Cynthia Ruchti for your skillful editing. Your major surgery and cosmetic work made me look good for my close-ups.

Maddie Scott, the 'knotty questions' image is pure genius.

For my small group and men's Bible study members for keeping me grounded. You're not at all impressed that I'm an author—and I appreciate that. Thanks.

And for you—you know who you are—for investing money and time to read this work. I appreciate you and pray that the time we spend together will be beneficial.

And thanks for sitting through the credits.

Introduction

> *Surely God is good to Israel,*
> *To those who are pure in heart!*
> *But as for me, my feet came close to stumbling,*
> *My steps had almost slipped.*
> *For I was envious of the arrogant*
> *As I saw the prosperity of the wicked.*
>
> *Surely in vain I have kept my heart pure*
> *And washed my hands in innocence;*
> *For I have been stricken all day long*
> *And chastened every morning.*
> Psalm 73:1-3, 13-14

Have you ever envied the arrogant? The prosperity of the wicked? I'll admit it. I have. And worse, I've wondered if I've kept my heart pure and hands innocent for nothing. Yep, it can feel like we're on a "Slip 'N Slide" coated with olive oil as we struggle with unanswered prayers, unfulfilled promises, and unpunished evil.

As we'll learn Asaph, one of the chief musicians of King David and King Solomon, watched the glorious rise of Israel—and its shameful decline and utter destruction. His psalms—50, 73-83—poetically and painfully chronicle his dark doubts, crippling confusion, and constant questions.

I nearly slipped on these three incidents:

Unanswered Prayer

"God, we're trusting you to heal Dave this morning." Fifty people from the church my wife and I attend knelt around the sixty-something man who had been diagnosed with an aggressive form of pancreatic cancer. Pastor Matthew had quoted James 5:14-15a:

> Are any of you sick? You should call for the elders of the church to come and pray over you, anointing you with oil in the name of the Lord. Such a prayer offered in faith will heal the sick, and the Lord will make you well (NLT).

The three hundred parishioner seated in the sanctuary agreed with hearty amens. As Dave was about to be anointed as prescribed in James, Pastor Matthew quietly asked him, "Dave, you know things don't look good. Do you know where you'll spend eternity?" After some hushed conversation back and forth, Dave confessed his need of a Savior and acknowledged that Jesus was his only hope. Everyone promised to continue praying.

A few days later, the church's Facebook page proclaimed the good news: Dave had accepted Christ as his Savior, and a scan revealed that he was *cancer free*! He was a personable individual who enjoyed sharing his newfound faith along with his wonder and amazement that the cancer was completely gone. Great rejoicing filled the church.

I too rejoiced, thinking, *Finally, an answer to a prayer for cancer healing after watching so many of my friends die—despite the anointings and prayers. And what a great faith-builder for the many brand-new Christians at the growing church. Thank you, Jesus.*

But just days after the great news, another Facebook post shared devastating news: The test was misread. Dave did indeed have a large mass on his pancreas and would need immediate surgery.

I nearly shouted at God. "We're praising you for a miracle—and it's all just a medical reporting error? This is going to destroy the fragile faith of new believers."

Again, we gathered around Dave and prayed for a healing—either supernatural or medical. And once again, social media kept the congregation informed as the ten-hour surgery dragged on throughout the day and prayers were sent heavenward for Dave.

> 6 P.M. URGENT PRAYER REQUEST: While removing the cancerous mass from Dave's abdomen, an artery was torn and a vascular surgeon has been called in for emergency repair. Thanks for your immediate prayers.
>
> 8 P.M. URGENT PRAYER REQUEST: Dave is VERY critical. Pastor Matthew returned to Indy and just had prayer over him asking that "God's Spirit would breathe life into Dave—either on this side or the other side of the Jordan." Thanks for your prayers.
>
> 8:25 P.M. TRAGIC NEWS. TRIUMPHANT NEWS REGARDING DAVE: Dave died this evening around 8:20 after complications following today's surgery for pancreatic cancer. He had recently accepted Christ as his Savior during prayer for his battle with pancreatic cancer, and is now cancer-free and safely Home.

The violent, up-and-down roller coaster ride—Dave's healing and salvation, the news of healing, the misread test, surgery which had been going well, and then his sudden death—went off the rails. And questions of *why* shook the congregation—and me. *Why had Dave died after he and the church had followed the biblical principles and believed with faith that he would be spared the prognosis of death? And why does God seem to toy with his children's emotions?*

Unfulfilled Promises

In the year 2000, I was hired by a Christian Internet company to serve as a writer and editor. I was paid well and praised God for the wonderful opportunity to support his work. Since my wife, as a pastor, had a parsonage, car, insurance, and salary provided, we lived on her income and benefits, while I gave away most of my salary to missions. I had been taught early on from Malachi 3:

> "Bring the whole tithe into the storehouse, so that there may be food in My house, and test Me now in this," says the Lord of hosts, "if I will not open for you the windows of heaven and pour out for you a blessing until it overflows" (3:10).

It was such a joy to be able to give generously as I had been given generously.

But then the dot.com bubble burst, my wife lost her job, and we found ourselves needing a loan—for the *exact* amount of what we "overpaid" on our tithe. (I know, you really can't over-pay God, but that was the feeling shaking my soul. Ever since I had placed a nickel of my fifty-cent allowance in the little plastic church in Sunday school, I had been taught, "You can't out give God." And yet, it seemed we had—right down to the last penny.

My wife was in tears, and I felt like a total failure as we signed the line on the loan document designated "debtor." It was as if my spiritual life flashed before my eyes.

What about Jesus' promise in Luke?

> [Jesus said] "Give, and it will be given to you. They will pour into your lap a good measure—pressed down, shaken together, *and* running over. For by your standard of measure it will be measured to you in return" (Luke 6:38).

It felt as if God had failed the test he dared his followers to give him in Malachi 3.

Unpunished Evil

As a Christian—and news junkie—my heart is broken each time I learn that the Islamic State In Iraq (ISIS or ISL) has targeted Christians in the Middle East. Since its formation in 2002, researchers at the University of Maryland estimate as of 2015, ISIS had committed 4,900 acts of terror resulting in at least 33,000 deaths, 41,000 injuries, and 11,000 prisoners. Its mode of operation includes suicide bombings, driving large trucks through crowds of people, beheading and torturing believers, raping young girls and women, and burning churches to the ground with doomed worshipers inside.

The slaughter of Christians is nothing new. In the twentieth century, more Christians died for their faith than in the first nineteen combined. Countries such as North Korea, Somalia, and Afghanistan brutally oppress those who simply love Christ.

My questions of unpunished evil erupted with the Vietnam War, with photos of naked children whose clothing had been burned off their bodies with napalm. That horror was followed by political scandals including the impeachment hearings against presidents Nixon and Clinton. Millions of Americans lost their pensions to corporate crimes. Human trafficking finally came out of the shadows revealing that twenty million men, women and children are victims of forced labor and sexual exploitation—some as young as four-years-old. *How long, Jesus, before you judge these torturers and murderers of your brothers and sisters? When will you avenge their blood? When are you coming back to restore the justice you have promised?*

I'm sure you have your stories and struggles with unanswered prayer, unfulfilled promises, and unpunished evil. In his psalms, Asaph honestly and transparently struggled. His psalms are angry, raw, and despondent, but they are also filled with white-knuckle trust in a good God during an ungodly time period. In these pages, we'll bravely and truthfully explore the depths of despair and the heights of hope. And there *is* hope.

Pause

For now, this may be as far as you wish to read in this book. You may be completely exhausted from the struggle and don't have the spiritual, mental, or emotional strength to consider the evidence and hear from eyewitnesses of how a loving God worked *seemingly* unanswered prayers, unfulfilled promises, and unpunished evil for the ultimate good (Romans 8:28). And that's okay. I've been there.

Please be assured you are not alone. The One who cried out, "My God! My God, why have you forsaken me?" holds you in his nail-scarred hands of love, comfort, and understanding.

> [He] understands our weaknesses, for *he faced all of the same testings we do*, yet he did not sin. So let us come boldly to the throne of our *gracious* God. There *we will receive his mercy, and we will find grace to help us when we need it most* (Hebrews 4:15-16 NLT, *author's emphasis*).

You may want to skip to Chapter 12, "God is Good," and simply meditate on his great love—even though you can't feel it at this time. Or put this book down and go take a long nap. (That's what God told Elijah to do as he was despairing of life.)

Then reach out to someone safe—who is not going to judge and condemn you for your current state—and share your struggles. You will discover that you are not alone with your questions. And there is hope. (I mentioned that already, right?)

Continue

If you choose to continue, let me caution you that this is not your typical Christian book. (If you've read any of my previous books, you already know I'm not your typical author.)

This book is more a collection of *evidence* than a book of *information.* I've tried my best to assemble and put in logical, sequential order convincing evidence from the Bible and godly authors as well as compelling eyewitness testimonies from Scripture and modern-day men and women how God uses our struggles to develop our faith. So, there's a little of my own thinking on the subject, but there is a *lot* of scriptures. In fact, I can imagine a reviewer criticizing this book as "hundreds of scriptures simply cobbled together." Let me assure you this accusation is not true. This book contains hundreds of scriptures *carefully and prayerfully* "cobbled together."

I pray that as I write—and as you read—the Holy Spirit will teach us both what is profitable and instructive as we explore God's compassionate working through our struggles. Let's humbly explore God's Word together.

Paul, who had the best theological schooling of his time, described God's working as a "mystery" five times in his letters.[1] I've described trying to comprehend God's mysterious ways as trying to teach algebra to algae. It's not that God is illogical—he's "super-logical" in a way our tiny skulls filled with a gooey tangle of neurons cannot possibly comprehend. This mystery goes back at least as far as the time of Asaph:

> Just as you do not know the path of the wind and how bones *are formed* in the womb of the pregnant woman, so you do not know the activity of God who makes all things (Ecclesiastes 11:5).

Martin Luther wrote, as if Jesus is speaking:

> Discipleship is not limited to what you can comprehend—it must transcend all comprehension. Plunge into the deep waters beyond your own comprehension, and I will help you to comprehend even as I do. Bewilderment is the true comprehension. Not to

know where you are going is the true knowledge. My comprehension transcends yours.[2]

As playwright and novelist, Somerset Maugham, notes, "A god that can be understood is not a god. Who can explain the Infinite in words?"[3]

So, as you read, keep in mind three important truths.

1. You are not alone in your struggles.

2. There is compelling evidence and a good amount of answers, but most of all encouragement as we personally deal with Asaph's—and our own—struggles.

3. There is hope. Many of the psalms start out with desperate despair, but before their conclusion, they catch a glimpse of hope and a new vision of God.

The Story Behind Asaph's Psalms

Asaph was the son of Berekiah, born into the house of Levi, the tribe given the honor and responsibility of serving as priests or mediators between Jehovah God and his people. Scripture notes that Berekiah was appointed Doorkeeper of the Ark of the Covenant.

Asaph came into leadership as the Ark is being returned to Israel (1 Samuel 6:7-2) after being captured by Philistines around 1000 B.C. (1 Samuel 4:3-11). The Ark contained the Ten Commandments, Aaron's rod, a jar of manna, the two stone tablets inscribed with the Ten Commandments, and the writings of Moses. Constructed at the command of God, according to his detailed instructions (Exodus 19:20; 24:18), it served as the focal point of worship for the Jewish people.

Aspah's specific assignment is spelled out in 1 Chronicles 16:4-5:

> He appointed some of the Levites *as* ministers before the ark of the Lord, even to celebrate and to

> thank and praise the LORD God of Israel . . . with musical instruments, harps, lyres; also Asaph *played* loud-sounding cymbals. . . .

This celebration would be the first of several high points in Jewish history witnessed first-hand by Asaph. After years in Egyptian captivity and attacks on their Promised Land—recorded in Joshua, Judges, 1 and 2 Samuel, 1 Kings, and 1 Chronicles—Israel was finally at peace. Israel was on the verge of Camelot, "The Great Society," Utopia, heaven on earth, and the zenith of worship of the God who had raised up a righteous king. Asaph rejoiced that:

> God is known in Judah; His name is great in Israel. His tabernacle is in Salem; His dwelling place also is in Zion. There He broke the flaming arrows, The shield and the sword and the weapons of war (Psalm 76:1-3).

The "Messiah" Has Come

Asaph may have been one of many who thought that Solomon was *the* promised Messiah, who would rule Israel forever in peace. In the Hebrew Bible, a *mashiach* or "messiah" is a king or high priest who has been ordained with holy anointing oil. While there were many anointed ones—even Cyrus the Great, King of Persia, is referred to as "messiah" (Isaiah 45:1)—the Jewish people were yearning for a future king of Israel from the line of David, who would rule with peace forever.

It all seemed to fit. Solomon was the son of David (although Solomon had his brother Adonijah killed to secure the throne). He was given divine wisdom (1 Kings 3:4-9) so that "People from every nation came to consult him and to hear the wisdom God had given him" (1 Kings 10:24). And, during this time, the scattered remnants of Israel returned to the holy city of Jerusalem.

No wonder Asaph felt that the Messianic age had arrived with the wise, anointed one on the throne and Israel becoming a world power.

The Temple Is Built

Asaph not only witnessed the return of the revered Ark of the Covenant to the Tent of Meeting, but was an eyewitness to the building of the magnificent Temple. "Magnificent" is an understatement. The building was 30 feet wide, 90 feet long, and 30 feet high. The interior walls and even the *floor* were covered in solid gold! (You can read the extravagant details in 1 Kings 6:18-34.)

CRASH!

But, just as Asaph had seen the rise of the kingdom, he now watched what would make an epic block-buster film with all the dramatic intrigue, seduction, adultery, murder, multiple wives, back-stabbing siblings conspiring for power, international intrigue, bloody battle scenes, spectacular settings, all accompanied with a sound track of thousands of singers and musicians. Hollywood has nothing on the Bible.

This tragic story provides the context of Asaph's sometimes dark and cynical poems. He had very good reasons to question everything about God, the government, and life itself as he witnessed . . .

Solomon's wealth at the citizen's expense. First Kings 10:14-29 documents the lavish and luxurious lifestyle Solomon demanded of the people he was anointed to serve.

His annual salary was twenty-five *tons* of gold. "This did not include the additional revenue he received from merchants and traders, all the kings of Arabia, and the governors of the land" (v. 10 NLT). In today's economy, with gold selling for over $1,250 per ounce, that would be equivalent to an annual base salary of more than one *billion* dollars.

His drinking cups were solid gold. "They were not made of silver, for silver was considered worthless in Solomon's day!" (1 Kings 10:21 NLT).

He also boasted a fleet of fourteen hundred chariots and twelve thousand horses.

Solomon's idolatry. As offensive as the king's "evil" and arrogant opulence—paid for by "oppressive" taxes by "the poor and destitute,"

Solomon's spiritual life must have been far more offensive to Asaph. First Kings 11 is perhaps one of the most heart-breaking chapters in all of Scripture. King Solomon "loved many foreign women...He had seven hundred wives, princesses, and three hundred concubines, and his wives turned his heart away...Solomon did what was evil in the sight of the LORD, and did not follow the LORD fully, as David his father *had done*."

> And God responded, "So the LORD said to Solomon, 'Because you have done this, and you have not kept My covenant and My statutes, which I have commanded you, I will surely tear the kingdom from you, and will give it to your servant.'" (Excerpted from 1 Kings 1-13 NLT).

Civil war breaks up the kingdom. After Solomon's death, Asaph witnessed the king's son, Rehoboam, not only continue heavy taxation to support his lavish lifestyle, but threaten even worse conditions. Jeroboam, who had served as Solomon's chief superintendent of forced labor and had fled to Egypt for political asylum, pleaded for relief. Rehoboam defiantly declared, "My father made your yoke heavy, but I will add to your yoke. My father chastised you with whips, but I will chastise you with scorpions" (1 King 12:14).

Incensed, the ten northern tribes rebelled in 932-931 B.C. and declared Jeroboam, from the tribe of Ephraim, king. But his rule would also prove equally ungodly. He disbanded the priesthood, set up golden calves as well as Asharah poles, which were used for worship of the Canaanite fertility god (1 Kings 12).

The Temple Is Destroyed. Eventually, the kingdom suffered complete destruction along with Solomon's magnificent Temple and palace. Asaph writes in Psalm 79:

> O God, the nations have invaded Your inheritance; They have defiled Your holy temple; They have laid Jerusalem in ruins. They have given the dead bodies

> of Your servants for food to the birds of the heavens, The flesh of Your godly ones to the beasts of the earth. They have poured out their blood like water round about Jerusalem; And there was no one to bury them. We have become a reproach to our neighbors, A scoffing and derision to those around us. How long, O Lord? Will You be angry forever? Will Your jealousy burn like fire? (vs. 1-5).

Is it any wonder that Asaph's psalms are filled with questions about unanswered prayer, unpunished evil, and unfulfilled promises?

We Are Not Alone

The psalms of Asaph teach us there are times when we may feel depressed, despondent, and even disturbed by the way God is apparently running his creation and dispensing justice. So, be comforted that you're in good company! A 2017 Barna survey revealed that 65 percent of American Christians have "experienced a time of spiritual doubt when [they] questioned what [they] believed about religion or God." These human emotions are a part of our natural perception of the divine supernatural workings of eternal God. Asaph lamented:

> So I tried to understand why the wicked prosper. But what a difficult task it is! (Psalm 73:16 NLT).

> Will the Lord reject forever? And will He never be favorable again? Has His lovingkindness ceased forever? Has *His* promise come to an end forever? Has God forgotten to be gracious, Or has He in anger withdrawn His compassion? (Psalm 77:7-9).

> O Lord God of Heaven's Armies, how long will you be angry with our prayers? You have fed us with sorrow and made us drink tears by the bucketful. You have made us the scorn of neighboring nations. Our enemies treat us as a joke (Psalm 80:4-6 NLT).

But the questions don't end in the psalms.

Jeremiah

While a full one-third of the psalms are classified as "laments," no one laments better than the prophet Jeremiah:

> I am the man who has seen affliction Because of the rod of [God's] wrath. He has driven me and made me walk In darkness and not in light. Surely against me He has turned His hand Repeatedly all the day. He has caused my flesh and my skin to waste away, He has broken my bones (Lamentations 3:1-4).

John the Baptist

John the Baptist, according to Jesus, was the greatest human who ever lived (Matthew 11:11). He was filled with the Holy Spirit before his birth, "leaped for joy" in vitro in the presence of the unborn Jesus (Luke 1:41, 45), lived a holy life, and baptized the Son of God. John saw "the Spirit descending" on Jesus (John 1) and "a voice out of the heavens" saying "This is My beloved Son, in whom I am well pleased." Great indeed!

And yet, when John the Baptist was thrown into prison for opposing Herod Antipas's adultery, he seemingly doubted what he had seen, heard—even what he himself had taught. He sent his disciples to

Jesus to ask, "Are you he who comes, or should we look for another?" (Matthew 11:3, Luke 7:20).

Jesus Christ

And most surprising, Jesus Christ, Eternal God-in-flesh, struggled!

> [Jesus said] "My soul is crushed with grief to the point of death" (Matthew 26:38a NLT).

> Being in agony he prayed more earnestly. His sweat became like great drops of blood falling down on the ground (Luke 22:44).

> At about three o'clock, Jesus called out with a loud voice, "*Eli, Eli, lema sabachthani?*" which means "My God, my God, why have you abandoned me?" (Matthew 27:46 NLT).

Paul and Luke

The apostle Paul, who penned nearly half of the New Testament, wrote, "For we do not want you to be unaware, brethren, of our affliction which came *to us* in Asia, that we were burdened excessively, beyond our strength, so that we despaired even of life" (2 Corinthians 1:8, *author's emphasis*). The "we" includes the author of the Gospel of Luke and Acts!

Contemporary Questioners

William Cowper, a great hymn-writer of the eighteenth century, is most famous for "There Is a Fountain Filled with Blood." And, yet, he attempted suicide numerous times before and *after* becoming a Christian and was later locked away in an asylum. In a letter to John "Amazing Grace" Newton he wrote in 1784:

> Loaded as my life is with despair, I have no such comfort as would result in the supposed probability of better things to come, were it once ended. . . . You will tell me that this cold gloom will be succeeded by a cheerful spring, and endeavor to encourage me to hope for a spiritual change resembling it—but it will be lost labour. Nature revives again, but a soul once slain lives no more.[4]

David Brainerd, the noted missionary to Native Americans, also described his longing for death, although he never recorded an attempt to take his own life:

> [I] was so overwhelmed with dejection that I know not how to live: I longed for death exceedingly, my soul was sunk in deep waters, and the floods were ready to drown me: I was so much oppressed that my soul was in a kind of horror. . . .[5]

> Indeed I seemed to feel wholly destitute of any happiness or hopes and expectations of happiness either in the present or coming world.[6]

> My whole soul was unspeakably bewildered and lost in myself. . . .[7]

A quick, but important note. The deep depression experienced by both Cowper and Brainerd may have been the result of clinical depression: a bio-chemical imbalance and not necessarily a spiritual issue.

I have struggled with clinical depression probably all my life, but was only diagnosed and treated at forty years old. For years, I was told by the church to simply have faith and think more positively—so I sunk deeper than depression into self-loathing. *I'm a faithless, hopeless excuse for a Christian.* I believed that lie for nearly forty years. Because it's a bio-chemical imbalance in the brain, exorcizing "stinkin' thinkin'" will not cure depression any more than it will cure diabetes, hypertension, or cancer. If you have felt depressed for more than two weeks—and especially if there appears to be no situational cause—see your doctor. There is help. There is hope. You do not have to live simmering in what famous preacher Charles Spurgeon called "a seething caldron of despair."

C. S. Lewis is arguably one of the greatest Christian writers of modern times. However, he wrote upon the death of his beloved wife and while "often screaming with the pain of osteoporosis":

> The moments at which you call most desperately and clamorously to God for help are precisely those when you seem to get none. Where is God? This is one of the most disquieting symptoms. . . . But go to Him when your need is desperate, when all other help is in vain, and what do you find? A door slammed in your face, and a sound of bolting and double bolting on the inside. After that, *silence.*[8]

Ann Voskamp, best-selling author of *One Thousand Gifts*, writes:

> C'mon, be honest. You sometimes gotta wonder if God's dropped his cosmic phone, lost track of the blasted time. I'm serious: "How long, for crying out loud, God. How long do we have to hope before you help? How long do we have to plead before you provide?"[9]

From My "In Box"

A woman recently responded to one of my hopeandhumor.org posts:

> I was one of five children born to parents in their teens. Only three of us survived. My dad was brutally attacked, his throat slit, and left for dead when I was three. He turned to alcohol and was never the same. My parents divorced, and Mom remarried when I was six, bringing two step-sisters into the family. When I was thirteen, my brother found my mom dead in the bathroom. I was left to parent my siblings as my step-dad became an alcoholic after Mom's death. When I was fifteen, my siblings and I were separated when willing relatives in different cities took us in after our "family" disintegrated. My sister attempted suicide, and my brother succeeded in taking his own life.
>
> I had accepted God as my "Everlasting Father" at age seven, and when I was in college I married a wonderful Christian man and finished college. We adopted my brother's daughter while he was in prison. At once she was diagnosed with a terminal muscle disease. She required total care, but had a sweet heart, great mind, an amazing attitude, and fast faith despite numerous hospital stays and brain surgery. She died at age nineteen. Two years after her death, my husband received a cancer diagnosis,

and I soon became a single mother with four young sons. During this time, I was also caring for my grandmother who lived with us for ten years.

By now, my faith was fragile, but I believed God's promises, held on, and waited—again—for God to redeem the losses.

I then met and married a man whose wife had died of cancer. We—and everyone in our lives—were thrilled that God had given us a second chance at love. During my widow years, I had kept a written record of what I believed were God's promises to me, and I clung to those like a drowning man to his lifeboat. When we married, I wrote those promises into a choral reading and our friends performed "Living Promises" using those verses. Eight years into our marriage, his massive stroke destroyed the life we had hoped for.

I no longer see the promises for today and now—perhaps I will see them in heaven. And, this loving (?) Everlasting Father, confuses me greatly. I trust by a moment by moment act of my will—but I no longer anticipate much good in this life. It hurts to hope.[10]

From My Journal

And here are some unedited excerpts from my journal

On the way to watch my two granddaughters, whom I love and adore, I drove past a cemetery and thought, *Lucky stiffs!* "Jesus, help me!" (January 2009)

I'm still struggling with unfulfilled promises in the Bible. We weren't able to pay our estimated taxes, we don't have health insurance, my gums are bleeding because I haven't been able to afford a dental appointment, and Lois said this morning, "Wait on bills. I don't think we have enough money in checking."

I don't understand! I sometimes wonder if God is on vacation and has left a raving lunatic in charge! (September 2009)

I am just so *tired*. Tired emotionally and spiritually from scraping bottom financially. Tired professionally from my books not selling well. Tired physically from forty-two radiation treatments for cancer. Tired from hearing that our son has lost his job and the grands are having health problems. It's just sucked all the energy out of me (March 2010).

How can someone who has a website called HopeAndHumor.org, gets rave reviews for his encouraging talks, and has written one-liners for a well-known comic be so stinkin' depressed?! (August 2010).

I trust that after reading these honest eyewitness testimonies, you can breathe a sigh of relief and realize, *I have not lost my faith simply because I have questions.* There is hope. Asaph chose to remember God's goodness in his despair:

> *I shall remember the deeds of the LORD; Surely*
> *I will remember Your wonders of old.*
> *I will meditate on all Your work*
> *And muse on Your deeds.*
> *Your way, O God, is holy;*
> *What god is great like our God?*
> *You are the God who works wonders;*
> *You have made known Your strength among the peoples.*
> *You have by Your power redeemed Your people. . . .*
> Psalm 77:11-15

Unanswered Prayer

1
Is Unanswered Prayer God's Fault?

Part One

Let Your compassion come quickly to meet us, For we are brought very low. Help us, O God of our salvation, for the glory of Your name; And deliver us and forgive our sins for Your name's sake.
Psalm 79:8b-9

On the kitchen wall in my boyhood home hung a plaque that promised "God Answers Prayer." Because of those words, reinforced in Sunday school and Bible story books, I got the idea that prayer was a 100-percent-guarantee, lifetime-warranty, you-must-be-completely-satisfied-or-your-money-back, over-night-delivery *promise*.

And so, as a first-grader, I prayed for a pony for my birthday . . . and didn't get it. I prayed for a pony for Christmas . . . and didn't get it.

During adolescence, I prayed that my face would clear up, and those prayers weren't answered either.

As I grew up, so did my prayers. They were far less selfish and included more altruistic requests such an end to the Vietnam War; for peace between the races as riots broke out across the nation; and—again—pleas for my face to clear up. No answers.

Now that I'm in the third quarter of life's game, I still have more losses than wins in my prayer bracket. Numerous friends have died of cancer—despite fervent prayers, fasting, and biblical practice of anointing with oil. Christian business leaders, who honored God in their treatment of employees and customers, went bankrupt. Despite prayers for safety, missionary friends have been kidnapped, raped, and killed. Friends who have faithfully spent their entire lives pastoring, are now in government-subsidized housing and trying to survive on food stamps.

Although it seems our "fervent" prayers are less than "effective" (James 5:16), we are commanded to pray: "In nothing be anxious, but in everything, by prayer and petition with thanksgiving, let your requests be made known to God" (Philippians 4:6).

In the Sermon on the Mount, Jesus assumes prayer is as natural as breathing or talking with a friend as he repeats "When you pray. . . ."

But have you ever felt that God has "slammed the door" on your prayers? Have you ever spent sleepless nights overwhelmed with longing for his help? Or have you been too distressed to even pray?

Asaph understands.

And so do I. To compound the psalmist's despair, he is taunted by memories of the good old days, long since ended. If we have experienced God's abundant blessings, the withdrawal of blessings make us cry out as Asaph did in Psalm 77:8, "Has God forgotten to be gracious?"

The cruel questions torment us because we believe that God *is* gracious and filled with compassion—and has promised to answer prayer: "And my God will supply all your needs according to His riches in glory in Christ Jesus" (Philippians 4:19).

So how do we reconcile these verses when there is no answer? We cry out with Asaph: "Have his promises permanently failed? Has

God forgotten to be gracious? Has he slammed the door on his compassion?" (Psalm 77:7-9).

The Nature of Prayer

In today's fast-food world, we often—well, at least I—sometimes treat prayer like the drive-through window at McDonalds. I scan the menu board of "promise verses," place my order, and then race the engine as I wait impatiently for my McPrayer "Happy Deal." But the prayer that Jesus taught his disciples to pray, has very little asking—or ordering—in it.

> "When you pray, don't be like the hypocrites who love to pray publicly on street corners and in the synagogues where everyone can see them. I tell you the truth, that is all the reward they will ever get. But when you pray, go away by yourself, shut the door behind you, and pray to your Father in private. Then your Father, who sees everything, will reward you.
>
> "When you pray, don't babble on and on as the Gentiles do. They think their prayers are answered merely by repeating their words again and again. Don't be like them, for your Father knows exactly what you need even before you ask him! Pray like this:
>
> "Our Father in heaven, may your name be kept holy. May your Kingdom come soon. May your will be done on earth, as it is in heaven. Give us today the food we need, and forgive us our sins, as we have for-

> given those who sin against us. And
> don't let us yield to temptation, but
> rescue us from the evil one.
>
> For yours is the kingdom and
> the power and the glory forever.
> Amen" (Matthew 6:5-13 NLT).

As a child, prayer in church always confused me. First, you had to drop your voice a full octave below your "real" voice to communicate with God.

Second, you had to bow your head as you "looked to the Lord in prayer." This was especially confusing, since I had always been taught God was "up there" and the devil was "down there." *Why are they looking to the Lord down there?*

Third, one spake verily with *thee*s and *thou*s with emotion and drama as if performing a soliloquy in a Shakespearean play. And, for the longest time, I thought God's name was "Wejust." "God, wejust come to you . . . And God, wejust ask that . . ."

And finally, prayer is not a public performance. And I'm going to go way out on a limb here by asking, "Does Jesus prohibit public prayer?" (Did I just write that?!) He *does* teach, "But when you pray, go away by yourself, shut the door behind you, and pray to your Father in private." I tend to be self-conscious when I am coerced to pray publicly. It's too easy for me to unconsciously speak to not just God, but the audience as well. So, inevitably, that prayer is not the honest, intimate, heart-to-heart communication I believe God desires.

We certainly have Jesus' precedence of sneaking off in the night to pray alone.

> After He had sent the crowds away, He
> went up on the mountain by Himself
> to pray; and when it was evening, He
> was there alone (Matthew 14:23).
>
> After bidding them farewell, He left for
> the mountain to pray (Mark 6:46).

And in his hour of deepest need, Jesus prayed alone.

> Then Jesus came with them to a place called Gethsemane, and said to His disciples, "Sit here while I go over there and pray." And He took with Him Peter and the two sons of Zebedee, and began to be grieved and distressed. Then He said to them, "My soul is deeply grieved, to the point of death; remain here and keep watch with Me."
>
> And He went a little beyond *them*, and fell on His face and prayed, saying, "My Father, if it is possible, let this cup pass from Me; yet not as I will, but as You will." And He came to the disciples and found them sleeping, and said to Peter, "So, you *men* could not keep watch with Me for one hour?" (Matthew 26:36-40).

Let's examine the model prayer Jesus gave us. And, in so doing, I think we'll answer the question: Is unanswered prayer God's fault?

Our Father in heaven, may your name be kept holy.

This is not the first time God is referred to as "Father."[11] Jesus is defining our relationship with God. He is a father with authority over his children who are commanded to "honor him" (Exodus 20:12). He is not the clerk in the drive-through window. He is not "the man upstairs." He is not a fishing buddy. But neither is he a capricious, vindictive, and morally-challenged god of the Greek and Roman pantheon. And he's not some nebulous "higher power" or "life force."

Jesus addressed his Father as *Abba*. Paul expanded on the concept: "For you have not received a spirit of slavery leading to fear again, but you have received a spirit of adoption as sons by which we cry out, 'Abba! Father!'" (Romans 8:15).

Abba is an Aramaic term of intimate love and affection between a father and child. A modern translation would render it "Daddy" or "Papa."

However, we are not only to view God as Daddy but as a completely holy being incapable of our human comprehension. It's a delicate balance. He is the holy ruler of the universe and an approachable parent to whom we can come to with our skinned lives.

And so, the first purpose of prayer is to put us in the proper relationship with Daddy/God. (Is that an amazing concept or what?)

May your Kingdom come soon. May your will be done on earth, as it is in heaven.

The second purpose is to align our desires with God's desires. He is not our personal online "wish list." It is not a time to educate God about our lives and the state of the world. A. W. Tozer writes:

> In all our praying . . . it is important that we keep in mind that God will not alter His eternal purposes at the word of a man. We do not pray in order to persuade God to change His mind. Prayer is not an assault upon the reluctance of God, nor an effort to secure a suspension of His will for us or for those for whom we pray. Prayer is not intended to overcome God and "move His arm." God will never be other than Himself, no matter how many people pray, nor how long nor how earnestly.
>
> What the praying man does is to bring his will into line with the will of God so God can do what He has all along been willing to do. Thus prayer changes the man and enables God to change things in answer to man's prayer.[12]

Soren Kierkegaard states it clearly: "Prayer does not change God, but it changes him who prays."[13]

Yes, prayer is a time to "ask" for needs, but most of all, a time to ask, "How can I do your will within the sphere of my influence today?"

Paul writes from his prison cell to the churches of Colossae and Laodecia:

> So we have not stopped praying for you since we first heard about you. We ask God to give you *complete knowledge of his will* and to give you *spiritual wisdom and understanding*. Then the way you live will always honor and please the Lord, and your lives will produce every kind of good fruit. All the while, you will grow as *you learn to know God better and better* (Colossians 1:9-10 NLT, *author's emphasis*).

Give us today the food we need.

Bread was a vital staple in the Palestinian diet, and so Jesus teaches:

> Now suppose one of you fathers is asked by his son for a fish; he will not give him a snake instead of a fish, will he? Or *if* he is asked for an egg, he will not give him a scorpion, will he? If you then, being evil, know how to give good gifts to your children, how much more will *your* heavenly Father give the Holy Spirit to those who ask Him?" (Luke 11:11-13).

Often preachers and writers stress that God gives us our "daily bread," and point to the way God have the Hebrews in the wilderness just the right amount of manna for each day, and if one tried to store it up (other than the day previous to the Sabbath), it would rot.

However, the Greek can also be translated, "Give us today our food for tomorrow." For someone who is a pathological planner, I like that rendering.

The point is that he will give us what we need. (Not necessarily what we *want*, but what we *need*.) In the Matthew 6 passage, Jesus reminds us that our "Father knows exactly what you need even before you ask him!"

Barbara Nicolossi is a Catholic sister who works in Hollywood as a screenwriter. She teaches we often don't know how to pray. Say, for instance, we hurt our foot. Should we pray for healing? Should we pray that this "thorn in the flesh" will humble us and make us more like Christ? Is there a way we can glorify God through our injured foot?

So, she suggests we simply pray, "Foot." I love that concept. We don't know what we *really* need, but God does. He even prays *for* us! Paul writes:

> [The] Spirit also helps our weakness; for we do not know how to pray as we should, but the Spirit Himself intercedes for *us* with groanings too deep for words; and He who searches the hearts knows what the mind of the Spirit is, because He intercedes for the saints according to *the will of* God (Romans 8:26-27).

Sometimes, we need to pray simply "Foot." Or maybe just "Spirit."

Forgive us our sins, as we have forgiven those who sin against us.

I'm going to spill a little more ink on this topic than the others, because I have seen the deadly damage unforgiveness and life-long grudges have caused in the lives of my friends. I have seen firsthand the truth of Anne Lamott's observation: "Not forgiving is like drinking rat poison and then waiting for the rat to die."

Unforgiveness will not only poison your soul, but will hinder your prayers. The Bible delivers some strong warnings on the subject:

> "Whenever you stand praying, forgive, if you have anything against anyone, so that your Father who is in heaven will also forgive you your transgressions" (Mark 11:25).
>
> "If you forgive others for their transgressions, your heavenly Father will also forgive you. But if you do not forgive others, then your Father will not forgive your transgressions" (Matthew 6:14-15).
>
> Let all bitterness and wrath and anger and clamor and slander be put away from you, along with all malice. Be kind to one another, tender-hearted, forgiving each other, just as God in Christ also has forgiven you (Ephesians 4:31-32).

Forgiveness doesn't hold benefits for only "spiritual" people. It provides some powerful physical and psychological benefits for every person.

Studies at John Hopkins School of Medicine have shown forgiveness lowers the risk of heart attack; lowers cholesterol levels; improves sleep; and reduces pain, blood pressure, levels of anxiety, depression and stress.

Dr. Karen Swartz at Hopkin's Mood Disorders Adult Consultation Clinic, notes:

> There is an enormous physical burden to being hurt and disappointed. Chronic anger puts you into a fight-or-flight mode, which results in numerous changes in heart rate, blood pressure and immune response. Those changes, then, increase the risk of depression, heart disease and diabetes, among oth-

er conditions. Forgiveness, however, calms stress levels, leading to improved health.[14]

However, there are some dangerous misconceptions of what forgiveness entails. Forgiveness is *not* condoning the offense, forgetting it ever happened, restoring trust, or promising reconciliation. And it is not easy. But it is a command straight from the mouth of Jesus. "Then Peter came and said to Him, 'Lord, how often shall my brother sin against me and I forgive him? Up to seven times?'" (Matthew 18:21).

Peter thought he was being extremely generous, because the rabbis taught one must forgive others three times. *I'll impress Jesus and answer seven!* Seven was considered the number of completion. God finished creation and took a day off in seven days. The leprous Naaman was commanded to dip in the Jordan River for healing seven times. Joshua and company were to march around the walls Jericho for seven days, and on the seventh, seven times. Seven was a number of fulfillment. *I've got the right answer, Jesus!*

"Jesus said to him, 'I do not say to you, up to seven times, but up to seventy times seven'" (Matthew 18:22).

In essence, Jesus is saying, "It's completion times infinity!" And forgiving someone four-hundred and ninety times does feel like forever.

But God is able to give us the grace and strength to forgive that way.

Yvonne told me her amazing story over a meal at a conference where I was speaking.

> My husband's unfaithfulness turned me bitter and self-righteous. It did not matter to me if he lived or died, went to heaven or hell, as long as he was out of my life. I joked that if Edward died before me, there would be a drive-by service. I would throw his ashes on the side of the road, and people could drive-by to pay their respects.

But somebody prayed for me, and God began to show me everything that was wrong with me. Not my husband. Me! I saw my bitterness and self-righteousness. I actually began to pray like my life depended on it for Edward and his girlfriend to get right with God as well.

It took a long time, but eventually my husband came to know God, he broke up with his girlfriend—who wrote me an apology—and Edward wanted to renew our wedding vows after twenty-nine years of an awful marriage.

I put on my wedding dress and, while Edward lay in his hospital bed [with a terminal illness], we renewed our vows. And this is the unbelievable part—with his ex-girlfriend and child as witnesses.

Jesus had completely, totally, unbelievably changed my attitude toward Edward. And even though I miss him so much, I know that God was taking all of the horrible experiences—not that He caused them—but was using these things to make me a better person.[15]

Yvonne's story is amazing, supernatural, God-given forgiveness.

Don't let us yield to temptation, but rescue us from the evil one.

I'll write much more about this in the next chapter, but for now know that we have an enemy who wants to use our times of unanswered prayers, unfulfilled promises, and unpunished evil to push us away from God rather than draw us closer to him. Stay tuned.

For yours is the kingdom and the power and the glory forever.

      Christ's model prayer begins with a reminder that God is our loving, holy Father. And it ends with the assurance that he has the power to bring about his glorious kingdom here on earth and forever.[16] And, so, Asaph gives thanks:

> *We give thanks to You, O God, we give thanks,*
> *For Your name is near;*
> *Men declare Your wondrous works.*
> Psalm 75:1

2
Is Unanswered Prayer God's Fault?

Part Two

> *My voice rises to God, and I will cry aloud;*
> *My voice rises to God, and He will hear me.*
> *In the day of my trouble I sought the Lord;*
> *In the night my hand was stretched out without weariness;*
> *My soul refused to be comforted.*
> Psalm 77:1-2

God always answers prayer. Always. I tried to demonstrate this truth in children's church. I taught God's answers are like a traffic light: red, yellow, and green: No. Slow. Go.

No

Sometimes we ask for things that are simply not good for us. My friend, Robert Hollinger, puts a spin on Jesus' promise in Luke 11:11-12:

> "Now suppose one of you fathers is asked by his son for a fish; he will not give him a snake instead of a fish, will he? Or *if* he is asked for an egg, he will not give him a scorpion, will he?"

Robert quips, "But sometimes we *ask* for snakes and scorpions."

And sometimes, God graciously answers no . . . but sometimes he answers a reluctant yes to our relentless nagging for something that is not good for us. Here are two dramatic biblical examples.

In Numbers 11, following God's dramatic actions to free the Israelites from Egypt, "the Israelites began to crave the good things of Egypt" (v. 4). Good things? They had been slave laborers under unbearable conditions. And when they grew too numerous, the Pharaoh had demanded the death of all Jewish male babies. And yet . . .

> The people of Israel also began to complain. "Oh, for some meat!" they exclaimed. "We remember the fish we used to eat for free in Egypt. And we had all the cucumbers, melons, leeks, onions, and garlic we wanted. But now our appetites are gone. All we ever see is this manna!" (vs. 4b-5).

According to Exodus 16:31, manna "was like coriander seed, white, and its taste was like wafers with honey." And while I'm sure it was healthy and nutritious, I probably would also have gotten tired of Honey Nut Cheerios three meals a day, seven days a week. The issue was not diet but disobedience toward God. Aspah wrote of the consequences:

> [The LORD] released the east wind in the heavens and guided the south wind by his mighty power. He rained down meat as thick as dust— birds as plentiful as the sand on the seashore! He caused the birds to fall within their camp and all around their tents. The people ate their fill. He gave them what they craved. But before they satisfied their craving, while the meat was yet in their mouths, the anger of God rose against them, and he killed their strongest men. He struck down the finest of Israel's young men (Psalm 78:26-31).

The place was called *Kibroth-hattaavah*, meaning "graves of gluttony." The incident—and judgment—is a powerful warning to take no for an answer. However, this lesson was forgotten four hundred years later when the leaders of Israel gathered and demanded of the prophet Samuel, "Now appoint a king for us to judge us like all the nations."

Keep in mind, for the entire history of the Jewish nation, God had been commanding them to *not* act like all the nations. I'm sure God was shaking his head, thinking, *What part of be "set apart" don't you people understand?* Reluctantly, he tells the prophet:

> "Listen to the voice of the people in regard to all that they say to you, for they have not rejected you, but they have rejected Me from being king over them. Like all the deeds which they have done since the day that I brought them up from Egypt even to this day— in that they have forsaken Me and served other gods—so they are doing to you also. Now then, listen to their

> voice; however, you shall solemnly warn them and tell them of the procedure of the king who will reign over them" (1 Samuel 8:7-9).

Yet Samuel tries to talk the leaders out of this rebellious request. "Let's think this through, guys. Remember that we-want-meat thing? Well, this is going to end just as badly. A king will take your children as slaves for his army and palace staff, he will tax you to death and you will regret the day you begged God for a king."

And yet—like stubborn toddlers—they stomped their feet and shouted louder, "Appoint a king for us to judge us like all the nations!"

So God gave them exactly what they wanted—despite his will and warnings. And just as he predicted—disaster.

Saul and David's conflicts raged. After Saul's death, a civil war broke out between his supporters and David's. David became king, but his son, Absalom, incited a coup against his father. More civil war. Solomon murdered his brother to become David's successor. Solomon imposed oppressive taxes on the people and led Israel into idolatry. More civil war broke out between Solomon's sons as to who would succeed their father . . .

Well, you get the point. Rinse and repeat. The people's demand for a king led to disasters of biblical proportions.

The Father, in his infinite wisdom, says no to those things which would be harmful to us physically, mentally, socially, or spiritually. I have seen too many pastors and writers obtain fame and fortune leading to a disastrous fall from grace betraying their spouses, neglecting their children, and being sucked into the rich and famous vortex.

My friend, Kathy Carlton Willis, is a poster child for *no* answers. She was diagnosed with autoimmune disease at age twenty-eight, has endured twenty surgeries—and counting—plus daily deals with symptoms of neuropathy (nerve pain), arthritis, dry mouth and eyes, bronchiectasis (lung problems), malignant hypertension, diabetes, plus an overactive inflammatory response which causes pain and swelling, as well as having to treat thyroid cancer with meds that cause flu-like symptoms. She, too, has received a no answer, but writes:

> When I was first diagnosed, I prayed for God to heal me. My church prayed.

Family and friends prayed. But the suffering continued, and instead it seemed like more health problems were actually piled on rather than removed.

God's Spirit inside me assured me that I would live a life of suffering, like Paul. God planned to do something far more through my health problems than through healing. He told me there would be times new medical conditions would surface and I could pray for him to take away the severity of it, but he would never remove it completely.

How do I cope? By knowing that God is in the pain as much as he's in removing pain. His presence provides peace. And any trial is temporary, compared to eternity. It's difficult to share this story with others because they want to fix me. They don't want to think there are times a loving God would allow his children to suffer. So, they assume either I lack faith or I have sin in my life. They put the failure of the prayer on me, rather than realizing God has his own way of dealing with our life trials. It's not that he doesn't care—he hurts for us when he sees us tormented with pain. But he knows it's not going to last forever, and will turn out for a much better good.

A few months ago, I had a simple surgery that resulted in serious complications. Others asked how I kept smiling during such personal turmoil. Even though my time in the hospital was miserable, the God-appointments were amazing! When people entered my room to do their jobs, God prompted me to say the right thing so they felt comfortable opening up about a burden. I got to deliver a dose of Jesus' grace before they left.

Only God could bring the hurting people to me when I was hurting and couldn't go to them. How rewarding, to be used for God's good and glory despite physical limitations. If you are going through a terrible circumstance, I'm here to share this fact: Trials polish the shine!

Whenever I have a challenge in life, people ask, "What did God teach you through it?" Pretty much every time, my reply is, "That his presence is enough for even this."

For whatever reason, God seems to use me in the *mess* rather than in the *best*. If that's the way he gets the most glory, I'm okay with that. My story is about how *big* he is despite my big problems. Whether in the best or the mess, I am blessed.[17]

Another friend, Sandi, owned the local Christian bookstore—and so had thousands of books filled with thousands of answers. Yet she writes:

As I reflect over my life, I've discovered that when it seemed God was not answering my prayers or fulfilling promises or punishing evil, he was working in my life and in others to show his sovereignty, his majesty, his love in ways I will never fully comprehend until I meet him face to face. So, like you, I ponder. Were my prayers answered in ways I did not grasp? Is he fulfilling his promises in ways yet to be revealed? Is evil being punished in ways I cannot see?

A dear friend, too young in my view to die, was dying of cancer, and many people were praying for his healing. Those were days when I talked to God while jogging. Each morning I would hit the road praying, my heart increasing its beat along with all the petitions I made. That day, my pleading came with tears for Bill. "Lord, you are the Great Physician, and I believe you can heal him; you did this many times by simply touching people. Please touch Bill and heal him completely, that he might live a long life with his family. He's too young to die."

Although I don't yet know the whole truth, God may have answered my prayer for Bill by healing him completely. Bill was given a new forever body as promised by Christ to us who are his. Or, he may have answered my prayer by showing me his mercy for Bill

> in another way to keep him something worse than cancer.
>
> But now, I'm struggling with questions again. Our dear son-in-law has a progressive brain disease that is robbing him of his speech, communication processes, and will eventually render him totally disabled and kill him in a long, slow manner. Am I praying for a miracle, for mercy, for healing? Oh, yes! Will God answer? He *can,* but *will* he?! So, I also pray for God to reveal his presence to him, to our daughter and granddaughters, to us, to give us strength as we daily struggle to walk this difficult journey. He *will* answer that prayer![18]

Sometimes, God seems to answer no. And other times . . .

Slow

My computer's "auto correct" insists that Asaph is spelled ASAP, meaning "as soon as possible." That's when we want our prayers answered! Yet Habakkuk 2:3 promises, "If [the answer] seems slow in coming, wait patiently, for it will surely take place. It will not be delayed."

I absolutely hate to wait. But Horatio Bonar encourages us:

> No prayer is lost. Praying breath is never spent in vain. There is no such thing as prayer unanswered or unnoticed by God, and some things that we count refusals or denials are simply delays.[19]

One of my most popular posts at hopeandhumor.org is "God Is Never Late . . . But He Sure Is *Slow.*" It lists five possible reasons why God may choose to ignore our human deadlines:

1. **To increase our faith**

Here's my theory: faith develops during the time—often a long time—between the human deadline and heavenly deliverance. For instance, in Matthew 8:24-27:

> And behold, there arose a great storm on the sea, so that the boat was being covered with the waves; but Jesus Himself was asleep. And they came to *Him* and woke Him, saying, "Save us, Lord; we are perishing!" He said to them, "Why are you afraid, you men of little faith?" Then He got up and rebuked the winds and the sea, and it became perfectly calm. The men were amazed, and said, "What kind of a man is this, that even the winds and the sea obey Him?"

I suspect we all have experienced those violent storms of life . . . and it seemed that Jesus was sound asleep! There have been too many times when bills are due—overdue—and our checking account is empty. In 1988, my wife was in seminary, my young children were in a Christian school, and our only income was from my writing and speaking. The only thing in our cupboard was a can of green beans. "Save us, Lord; we are perishing!"

God seemed to say, "I just want you to praise me today. Not to make passionate petitions. Not to make calls to hustle work. Not to get a cash advance on the credit card. Just praise me, and watch me work."

I made a list of everything for which I could praise God: salvation, a godly wife called into ministry, two bright, healthy kids, a beautiful home in the 'burbs—which we bought when we both had good-paying "real" jobs, the opportunity to write books and articles . . . and the list went on and on.

This was during the dark ages when paper bank statements were snail-mailed to your home. At three o'clock, I heard the mail slot clink and the mail hit the floor. Our statement noted our checking account had $500 more than I thought we had (I am a writer, not an accountant). Also in the mail: a check for $1,000 from the university where I was writing advertising copy!

Like the rain-soaked disciples going under for the third time, I was "amazed." (I am such a slow learner!) God has to continue to remind of "What kind of man is this? Even the winds and the waves obey him!"

2. To increase our vision

The disciples' "vision" of Jesus had changed from "Who is this man?" to "You are the Son of God." They now had a vision of his power, his providence, and his parenting philosophy.

Over and over, God has taken me through this faith-building gap between the human deadline and heavenly deliverance. He uses these times of waiting to increase our vision.

3. To increase our testimony

As I read biblical stories, I'm convinced that God loves drama. The story of the three Hebrew men in the fiery furnace probably wouldn't have made it into the Bible if Shadrach, Meshach and Abednego had simply overpowered the guards and high-jacked a chariot. Somehow "Daniel and the Hung Jury" just doesn't have the impact of "Daniel in the Lions Den." And "Jesus Feeding Twelve Disciples with a Bucket of KFC" is not exactly amazing.

4. To increase God's glory

The story of Lazarus' resurrection is a classic story of waiting,

> Now a certain man was sick, Lazarus of Bethany, the village of Mary and her sister Martha. It was the Mary who anointed the Lord with ointment, and wiped His feet with her hair,

whose brother Lazarus was sick. So the sisters sent *word* to Him, saying, "Lord, behold, he whom You love is sick." But when Jesus heard *this*, He said, "This sickness is not to end in death, but for the glory of God, so that the Son of God may be glorified by it." Now Jesus loved Martha and her sister and Lazarus (John 11:1-5).

Our first reaction maybe, *Well, he had a funny way of showing love.* Jesus deliberately waited two days before leaving for Bethany. An unattributed author in *Streams in the Desert*, writes:

> In the forefront of this marvelous chapter stands the affirmation, "Jesus loved Martha, and her sister, and Lazarus," as if to teach us that at the very heart and foundation of all God's dealings with us, however dark and mysterious they may be, we must dare to believe in and assert the infinite, unmerited, and unchanging love of God. Love permits pain.[20]

In fact, by the time Jesus arrived, his friend had already been in the tomb four days. Martha cried out, "Lord, if You had been here, my brother would not have died. Even now I know that whatever You ask of God, God will give You" (11:22). Even in her despair, she still had faith in Jesus' love and power. Jesus and Mary had the same discussion.

"Jesus said, 'Remove the stone.' Martha, the sister of the deceased, said to Him, 'Lord, by this time there will be a stench, for he has been *dead* four days'" (11:39).

It's significant that he has been in the tomb for four days, as many of the Jewish teachers believed that the dead person's soul didn't leave the body until three days after death.

[But] Jesus raised His eyes, and said, "Father, I thank You that You have heard Me. I knew that You always hear Me; but because of the people standing around I said it, so that they may believe that You sent Me." When He had said these things, He cried out with a loud voice, "Lazarus, come forth." The man who had died came forth, bound hand and foot with wrappings, and his face was wrapped around with a cloth. Jesus said to them, "Unbind him, and let him go."

Therefore many of the Jews who came to Mary, and saw what He had done, believed in Him (John 11:41-45).

Now, what would have given Jesus more glory? Healing Lazarus from a serious illness or raising him from the dead? The delay—over four days—brought Jesus glory and "many of the Jews believed in him."

And one more important reason for God to delay an answer to prayer:

5. **To increase our compassion**

One reason for God's incredible slowness is his incredible love: "The Lord is not slow about His promise, as some count slowness, but is patient toward you, not wishing for any to perish but for all to come to repentance" (2 Peter 3:9).

Over twenty-five years ago, while writhing on an x-ray table with a firmly lodged kidney stone, I was praying for Jesus to return right then and there!

How many people do you think have come to Christ during those twenty-five years? According to one missions organization, 174,000 receive Christ as their Savior every day. So, that's 6,351,000 each year. Multiply that by twenty-five and you get 158,775,000 converts since my desperate prayer! If God had answered my prayer in November 1991, not one of those 158 million people would have known eternal life!

Part of God's delay, then, is his holy love that is so much greater than our human lusts. And we become more compassionate after we have been through that time between human deadlines and divine deliverance.

Go

Finally, if something is good for us and good for us now, the prayer light turns green.

My wife and I had a really heart-breaking experience in a church we were pastoring. So, when I wrote *Squeezing Good Out of Bad,* I included the gory details in a not so gracious manner. When the book proposal kept coming back from publishers, I ignored the yellow light and blew right through the divine intersection by publishing it myself.

A few years later—again, I am such a slow-learner—God began to make me feel uncomfortable about what I had written about the church. I "squeezed" the venom from it, while still telling how God graciously worked good out of the situation. Only then did a publisher come to me asking to publish it.

So, I'm learning to take yellow lights as seriously as red. I'm learning to wait—there's that word again—for a solid green light.

I appreciate how my friend, Mary Lynne Potma-Cameron, is open to no, slow, or go as she reaches what she calls "the bottom of the barrel" as far as cancer treatments. She writes on her blog:

> Unfortunately, there's one brief treatment I can take, then one that depends on how long I do okay with it. After that, my only options would be the few trials that my doctor thinks I might be able to qualify for. If I just look at the science, it sounds horrible.

But as the shock of the last few days has worn down, I've gone back to the God who is with me. Yes, it's possible that I'll get to see him in person earlier than expected. But he is in charge. He keeps giving stuff to me to do. He keeps educating me. I don't know exactly what his plans are, but he does. And despite how my heart may feel from day to day, I know that he loves me. He loves me deeply. He also has a loving imagination for what he would have me do. He could have used the first medication I was put on to give me years and years or he can suddenly keep me going for decades after all the medications have worn out.

What he does doesn't have to make sense. He can take me home tomorrow and then, somehow, what he's had me do so far will impact others in some way even though I'm not here. Or, he can use me in person to help others. Maybe I'll even get the opportunity to go speak to people here, there, and everywhere about his awesome love.

In any case, I don't know what his plans are. But I trust him. And trusting my future and even today to him makes each day so much easier. No matter what the crumminess is that can be so easily overwhelming, God is so much bigger and so much more powerful than any of the negative stuff in my life. He's also so much bigger than the stuff in your life. Leave it in his hands and then start getting excited about the awesome things he may have in store for you![21]

Don't Know

While living in New Castle, Pennsylvania, we awoke one morning to find our back door kicked in and laying on the kitchen floor. I was serving as interim pastor and, since we were only there for six months, the church had furnished the vacant parsonage with second-hand furniture complete with a recliner repaired with duct tape and a black and white TV with a coat hanger for an antenna. I joked, "The burglars must have looked around and thought, *Man, there's nothing in here worth five to ten years for breaking and entering*, because not one thing was missing."

I thought it was a funny story, but when I told it to my friend, Crystal, instead of laughing, her eyes widened. "What year were you there?" 1979. Now she looked concerned. "When in 1979?" I think the break-in was January or February. She looked straight into my eyes. "My uncle was shot and killed by burglars in New Castle in the winter of 1979."

My heart started pounding as I realized—thirty-five years later—the burglars who kicked in our door may have been the very same ones who killed Crystal's uncle!

I'm still shaken by the question, Why did God spare me, my wife and one-year-old daughter?"

So, there's part of me that rejoices when people praise God that he cured them of cancer, and another part that questions why did so many—my father, my mother-in-law, and too many friends—die a painful, prolonged death. I almost cringe when Christians testify that God spared them a crash with a drunk driver, when a good friend's godly parents were killed by a drunk driver. And I wonder why we were spared, and my friend's uncle was murdered. In our church, two families' homes were spared serious damage from tornadoes. Yet another family had their home destroyed by the twister. Almost as soon as they were able to move back into their restored house, lightning struck and fire destroyed it. I fear that these positive testimonies only create questions for the many—maybe, more—times God didn't answer in a positive way.

Perhaps, I should add to "Red: no, Yellow: slow, and Green: go" this response: "The light is out: don't know." I have to believe that God is sovereign, but that he also allows freewill for his creations to do evil: to rape, to murder, to drive drunk. I understand—begrudgingly—that we live in a fallen world filled with disease and natural disasters.

So, I'm slowly learning to "Be anxious for nothing, but in everything by prayer and supplication with thanksgiving let your requests be made known to God" (Philippians 4:6-7). Asaph had learned that secret:

"Offer to God a sacrifice of thanksgiving
And pay your vows to the Most High;
Call upon Me in the day of trouble;
I shall rescue you, and you will honor Me."
Psalm 50:14-15

3

Is Unanswered Prayer Someone Else's Fault?

*"Let there be no strange god among you;
Nor shall you worship any foreign god.
"I, the L*ORD*, am your God,
Who brought you up from the land of Egypt;
Open your mouth wide and I will fill it.
"But My people did not listen to My voice,
And Israel did not obey Me.
"So I gave them over to the stubbornness of their heart,
To walk in their own devices.
"Oh that My people would listen to Me,
That Israel would walk in My ways!"*
Psalm 81:9-13

Is unanswered prayer someone else's fault? Sometimes.

People can affect our prayers

American Christianity tends to be very individualistic: "Just Jesus and me!" But throughout Scripture, God works through his *people*. Notice that one of the most famous prayers of the Bible is to be prayed by his "people."

> Then if my people who are called by my name will humble themselves and pray and seek my face and turn from their wicked ways, I will hear from heaven and will forgive their sins and restore their land (2 Chronicles 7:14 NLT).

The prayer is for *people* to humble themselves, seek God's face, and turn from *their* wicked ways. Then he will forgive *their* sins and heal *their land*.

Notice, too, that Jesus' model prayer is plural: "Our Father," "Give us," "forgive our sins," "don't let us," and "rescue us" (Matthew 6).

Yep, there's one major issue: People have freewill. Although God is sovereign, his creations are free to make choices. People kept even some of Jesus' prayers from being answered. In his last recorded prayer before his death and resurrection, he prays that his disciples "May all be one; even as You, Father, *are* in Me and I in You, that they also may be in Us, so that the world may believe that You sent Me" (John 17:18-23).

It appeared that Jesus' prayer was answered in the early chapter of the Book of Acts: "These all with *one mind* were continually devoting themselves to prayer, along with *the* women, and Mary the mother of Jesus, and with His brothers (Acts 1:14, *author's emphasis*).

> When the day of Pentecost had come, *they were all together in one place* (Acts 2:1, *author's emphasis*).

> And all those who had believed were together and had all things in common; and they began selling their property and possessions and were sharing them with all, as anyone might have need. Day by day continuing with one mind in the temple, and breaking bread [as] from house to house, they were taking their meals together with gladness and sincerity of heart, praising God and having favor with all the people (Acts 2:44-47a).

Unfortunately, the holy harmony turned to nearly two thousand years of church fights, splits, and schisms (Catholic, Orthodox, Protestant, etc.). In 1900, the Center for the Study of Global Christianity estimated there were sixteen hundred denominations—not including varieties of Catholic and Orthodox churches. By 2000, the number of denominations jumped to thirty-four thousand, and in 2012 to forty-three thousand. That's a 2,125 percent increase in a little over one hundred years.

While Jesus' prayer has not been answered throughout church history, it *will be* fulfilled in eternity when "a great multitude . . . like the sound of many waters [and] mighty peals of thunder" will praise Him as one (Revelation 19:6).

There seem to be four ways God works in this world:

1. God's will, God's way

Doing what God wants always leads to the best results.

The story of Noah is good example. "Noah found favor in the eyes of the LORD. [He] was a righteous man, blameless in his time [and] walked with God" (Genesis 6:8, 9).

"Noah did according to all that the LORD had commanded him" (v. 7:5). He built an ark to the precise specs and filled it with his family and seven of each ceremonially "clean" animal and two of every "unclean" animal. And so his family and species of animals were spared the great flood.

But sometimes, humans can do God's will—despite their ungodly ways.

2. God's will, humans' way

I mentioned a few pages earlier a heart-breaking experience Lois and I had at a church. It forced us to leave the church we loved where we were loved. But God used the actions of a few humans to move us.

It wasn't until two years later that we could rejoice in God's will. We were shocked to learn that our daughter's husband was cheating on her.

If we had continued at the church, we would have been one hundred miles from our daughter and her two adorable girls. We wouldn't have been close by to respond to the numerous calls for help. To be there as she packed up their things to move out of her "dream house," to be there for the emotionally-charged divorce, to be there for "dad/daughter dates," and to be there when she would stop by our house simply for a hug.

I am so grateful that God's will was accomplished—even if by human means!

3. Human's will, human's way

And even human's will by human's way can be redeemed by God. Our daughter, Faith, has grown into such a strong woman and follower of Jesus. She's been an amazing single mom to her daughters, and has excelled in her career as a licensed clinical social worker. She posted her original observation on Facebook: "When God closes a door . . . he just knocks the whole side of a house out and opens up an amazing view!" I couldn't be prouder of her.

Dallas Willard notes, "Nothing irredeemable has happened to us or can happen to us on our way to our destiny in God's world."[22]

4. Humans' will, God's way

When I was growing up, our next-door neighbors smoked and didn't go to church. And they went to parties where there was—

Gasp!—alcohol. Of course, in the legalistic environment in which I grew up, I believed they could not possibly be godly people.

And yet, they were some of the most loving, generous people I had ever met. They may have been human, but they still reflected the image of God in which they were created. And so, I am grateful for humans who do God's work in caring for "the least of these." Many of the world's most philanthropic individuals do not profess to know Jesus—and yet they are carrying out his work to feed the hungry, clothe the naked, care for strangers, and visit prisoners (Matthew 25:31-46).

Finally, there is someone who can affect our prayers.

Satan can affect our prayers

"Watch out for your great enemy, the devil. He prowls around like a roaring lion, looking for someone to devour" (1 Peter 5:8 NLT).

There are two examples in the Bible of the enemy explicitly interfering with God's plans. In Daniel, we find:

> [The angel] said to me, "O Daniel, man of high esteem, understand the words that I am about to tell you and stand upright, for I have now been sent to you." And when he had spoken this word to me, I stood up trembling. Then he said to me, "Do not be afraid, Daniel, for from the first day that you set your heart on understanding this and on humbling yourself before your God, your words were heard, and I have come in response to your words. But the prince of the kingdom of Persia was withstanding me for twenty-one days; then behold, Michael, one of the chief princes, came to help me, for I had been left there with the kings of Persia (10:11-13).

The book of Daniel is filled with visions and allegories, but it seems that an angel was instantly dispatched with a message from God to Daniel, but was delayed for twenty-one days by the "prince of Persia." Most commentators believe the prince to be Satan. The archangel Michael was sent to release this angel, who then continued on his way to Daniel.

We see another example of Satan interfering in the New Testament: "For we wanted to come to you—I, Paul, more than once—and *yet* Satan hindered us" (1 Thessalonians 2:18).

The good news, however, is that God is sovereign even over Satan. The ruler of the universe seems to have Satan on a short leash. We see this in the story of Job. There are so many clues packed into this passage:

> One day the members of the heavenly court came to present themselves before the Lord, and the Accuser, Satan, came with them. "Where have you come from?" the Lord asked Satan.
>
> Satan answered the Lord, "I have been patrolling the earth, watching everything that's going on."
>
> Then the Lord asked Satan, "Have you noticed my servant Job? He is the finest man in all the earth. He is blameless—a man of complete integrity. He fears God and stays away from evil."
>
> Satan replied to the Lord, "Yes, but Job has good reason to fear God. You have always put a wall of protection around him and his home and his property. You have made him prosper in everything he does. Look how rich he is! But reach out and take away

> everything he has, and he will surely curse you to your face!"
>
> "All right, you may test him," the LORD said to Satan. "Do whatever you want with everything he possesses, but don't harm him physically." So Satan left the LORD's presence (1:6-12 NLT).

Notice that Satan and other heavenly beings are required to "present themselves before the LORD." The Hebrew word *yâtsab* means to "offer" or "present self." Some commentators render this "to give an account."

Satan is subservient to God. There is only one lord of lords, king of king, supreme ruler of the universe. Satan's power and activities are limited by God.

Satan must gain permission to harm Job. God had placed "a wall of protection around [Job] and his home and his property." The enemy could not harm Job without the permission of God.

We see this same "agreement" in The Gospels:

> [Jesus said,] "Simon, Simon, behold, Satan has demanded *permission* to sift you like wheat; but I have prayed for you, that your faith may not fail; and you, when once you have turned again, strengthen your brothers" (Luke 22:31–32, *author's emphasis*).

Jesus allowed Satan "permission" to tempt Simon Peter, but Jesus also prayed that Peter's faith would not fail. And Peter was redeemed after his denial of Christ.

At least in these two cases, Satan must gain God's express permission to try his children. So, does this mean, as some teach, "that nothing happens to God's children that he does not allow?" I'm not sure we can make the leap. I have no clue if God allows, causes, or takes a hands-off approach to specific events our lives. However, I do firmly, completely, emphatically believe that God *redeems* everything that happens to us. Romans 8:28-29 promises:

> And we know that God causes all things to work together for good to those who love God, to those who are called according to *His* purpose [which is]… *to become* conformed to the image of His Son…(*author's emphasis*).

God's purpose will be accomplished. However, Satan is determined to disrupt God's purpose in any way he can.

But Job—nearing the end of his trial—triumphantly declares to God: "I know that you can do all things, and that no purpose of yours can be thwarted" (Job 42:2).

Isaiah would agree: "The Lord of Heaven's Armies has spoken—who can change his plans? When his hand is raised, who can stop him?" (Isaiah 14:27).

Satan has a strategy and spiritual beings (fallen angels/demons) determined stop us from being "conformed to the image of his Son."

And it is a subtle, subversive plan because "Satan masquerades as an angel of light. It is no great thing therefore if his servants also masquerade as servants of righteousness, whose end will be according to their works" (2 Corinthians 11:14-15). This is why we are warned "don't believe every spirit, but test the spirits, whether they are of God" (1 John 4:1).

This is why Paul urges:

> Put on all of God's armor so that you will be able to stand firm against all strategies of the devil. For we are not fighting against flesh-and-blood enemies, but against evil rulers and authorities of the unseen world, against mighty powers in this dark world, and against evil spirits in the heavenly places (Ephesians 6:11-12 NLT).

You are from God, little children, and have overcome them; because greater is He who is in you than he who is in the world (1 John 4:4).

Asaph rejoices that God, indeed, is our strength, freedom, and salvation:

Sing praises to God, our strength.
Sing to the God of Jacob.
Sing! Beat the tambourine.
Play the sweet lyre and the harp.
Blow the ram's horn at new moon,
and again at full moon to call a festival!
For this is required by the decrees of Israel;
it is a regulation of the God of Jacob.
He made it a law for Israel
when he attacked Egypt to set us free.
I heard an unknown voice say,
"Now I will take the load from your shoulders;
I will free your hands from their heavy tasks.
You cried to me in trouble, and I saved you. . . .
Psalm 81:1-7

4
Is Unanswered Prayer My Fault?

*O God, restore us
And cause Your face to shine upon us, and we will be saved.
O LORD God of hosts,
How long will You be angry with the prayer of Your people?
You have fed them with the bread of tears,
And You have made them to drink tears in large measure.
You make us an object of contention to our neighbors,
And our enemies laugh among themselves.
O God of hosts, restore us
And cause Your face to shine upon us, and we will be saved.*
Psalm 80:3-7

If we aren't healed, it is our fault?

The apostle Paul would strongly disagree. He suffered with a thorn in the flesh (2 Corinthians 12:7-10), an unspecified "bodily illness" that was a "trial" and loathsome (Galatians 4:13-14), as well as bad eyes (Galatians 4:15).

Paul's co-workers would also object: Timothy with his stomach problems and "frequent ailments" (1 Timothy 5:23), as well as Trophimus who Paul left "ill at Miletus." (2 Timothy 4:20).

The question of why some people are healed and some are not is challenging, to say the least. It appears that God can be glorified both through physical healing as well by those who glorify him through their afflictions. Kathy Willis shared this truth earlier. Joni Eareckson Tada has used her quadriplegia to encourage millions with disabilities. And Billy Graham continues to be a powerful influence despite unhealed fluid on the brain, Parkinson disease, and cancer.

God has a plan for us that is "good, pleasing, perfect" (Romans 12:2). That plan may include being healed or not. And in many cases, those whom Henri Nouwen call "wounded healers," have a much greater ministry bearing their thorn in the flesh than those with miraculous healing. The result, no matter which, is that God gives us his grace to glorify him in our current state. And we will all be gloriously healed in eternity.

That said, there *are* ways we can hinder God answering prayer:

Anger, dissension

Anger hinders prayer. Jesus notes the seriousness of anger by listing it as the motive for murder (Matthew 5:21-22). In Ephesians 4, Paul warns that anger "grieves" the Holy Spirit (v. 30) and gives "the devil an opportunity" for unrighteousness (v. 27). "Let all bitterness and wrath and anger and clamor and slander be put away from you, along with all malice"(v. 30).

The apostle writes, "Therefore I want the men in every place to pray, lifting up holy hands, without wrath and dissension" (1 Timothy 2:8).

Dishonoring spouse

God is very clear that a husband's mistreatment of his wife can also hinder prayer. When our relationships with others are not godly, it affects our relationship with God. Both the Old and New Testaments provide specific warnings:

> "You cover the altar of the LORD with tears, with weeping and with groaning, because He no longer regards the offering or accepts *it with* favor from your hand. Yet you say, 'For what reason?' Because the LORD has been a witness between you and the wife of your youth, against whom you have dealt treacherously, though she is your companion and your wife by covenant" (Malachi 2:13-15).

> In the same way, you husbands must give honor to your wives. Treat your wife with understanding as you live together. She may be weaker than you are, but she is your equal partner in God's gift of new life. Treat her as you should so your prayers will not be hindered (1 Peter 3:7 NLT).

Who knew that throwing your dirty clothes in the hamper instead of on the floor—like your wife has asked you to do the past ten years—could improve your prayer life!

Disobedience

Throughout the story of King David and his descendants, we see disaster after disaster "because they did not obey the voice of the LORD their God, but transgressed His covenant, *even* all that Moses the servant of the Lord commanded; they would neither listen nor do *it* (2 Kings 18:12).

The history of Israel makes it clear that "God detests the prayers of a person who ignores the law" (Proverbs 28:9 NLT).

The only prayer of a disobedient person that God promises to hear is the prayer of repentance.

"Beloved, if our heart does not condemn us, we have confidence before God; and whatever we ask we receive from Him, because we keep His commandments and do the things that are pleasing in His sight" (1 John 3:21-22).

"This is the confidence which we have before Him, that, if we ask anything according to His will, He hears us" (1 John 5:14).

Obedience is a vital component to prayer.

Doubt

Faith certainly plays a role in answers to prayer. "But he must ask in faith without any doubting, for the one who doubts is like the surf of the sea, driven and tossed by the wind" (James 1:6).

When a Roman centurion confidently believed Jesus could heal his servant, Jesus responded: "'Truly I say to you, I have not found such great faith with anyone in Israel. . . . Go; it shall be done for you as you have believed.' And the servant was healed that *very* moment" (Matthew 8:10, 13).

The woman who touched the hem of Jesus' robe was hoping to be cured after years of hemorrhaging. "He said to her, 'Daughter, your faith has made you well; go in peace and be healed of your affliction'" (Mark 5:34).

However, there is grace for those who don't seem to possess a Spirit-given gift of faith (1 Corinthians 12:9). A desperate father brought his son to Jesus:

> "Teacher, I brought You my son, possessed with a spirit which makes him mute; and whenever it seizes him, it slams him *to the ground* and he foams *at the mouth*, and grinds his

teeth and stiffens out. . . . It has often thrown him both into the fire and into the water to destroy him. But if You can do anything, take pity on us and help us!" And Jesus said to him, "'If You can?' All things are possible to him who believes." Immediately the boy's father cried out and said, "I do believe; help my unbelief" (Mark 9:17-18, 22-24).

I'm afraid that would be me. I *do* believe. I really do. I have put my trust in the Son as my Savior, the Spirit as my power to live a righteous life, and the Father to direct my life. I do believe, but it's not perfect faith.

I am grateful that God's grace will accept my tiny "mustard seed" of belief (Matthew 17:19-21).

Estrangement from Jesus

Jesus promises, "If you remain in me and my words remain in you, you may ask for anything you want, and it will be granted!" (John 15:7 NLT). This promise is written in the context of Jesus being the grape vine and his followers being the branches growing out from it.

Our spiritual lives depend on this intimate connection with Christ. His life sap flows into and through us causing us to become one in his character. Our prayers are now motivated from the love of Christ within us. We now want what Christ wants, and as a result *those* prayers are answered.

Evil

As mentioned earlier, the only prayer of a disobedient person that God promises to hear is the prayer of repentance. We have God's Word on it:

"So when you spread out your hands *in prayer*, I will hide My eyes from you;

> Yes, even though you multiply prayers, I will not listen. Your hands are covered with blood.
>
> Wash yourselves, make yourselves clean; Remove the evil of your deeds from My sight. Cease to do evil" (Isaiah 1:15-16).

Laziness

You probably know people who, when complimented for a great job, answer, "It wasn't me. It was all God." I'm reminded of a story of a believer who told a friend with a beautiful flower garden, "God has given you a beautiful flower garden."

The gardener replied, "Well, it was just a lot of weeds when God had it all by himself."

We can't create beautiful flowers, but we can create beautiful gardens. God will not do something that we can do. We find several examples in Scripture.

In Luke 9, we read the miracle of Jesus feeding five thousand men—not to mention women, children and teenage boys—with just five loaves and two fish.

Notice that Jesus said to them, "*You* give them something to eat" and then delegated tasks:

You feed them.

You tell them to sit down in groups of fifty.

You distribute the food. (It would have been morning before Jesus could have personally served the crowd!)

You pick up the leftovers.

Only Jesus could multiply a boy's small lunch to serve a banquet to possibly ten thousand hungry people.

We see the same cooperation between the miraculous and mundane in the raising of Lazarus from the dead.

> Now [the tomb] was a cave, and a stone was lying against it. Jesus said, "Remove the stone."

> [Then Jesus] cried out with a loud voice, "Lazarus, come forth." The man who had died came forth, bound hand and foot with wrappings, and his face was wrapped around with a cloth. Jesus said to them, "Unbind him, and let him go" (John 11:38, 43-44).

If you're the Son of God and can raise a dead man who been in the tomb for four days, you can certainly beam him right through the stone wearing a fresh robe and clean underwear. But Jesus enlists his disciples to move the huge stone from the opening of the cave, and when Lazarus is brought to life, to strip off the burial clothes binding him.

God never answers a prayer that we can fulfill with our own effort. He will gladly do what only he can do, if we will do what we can do.

Hypocrisy

> "When you pray, you are not to be like the hypocrites; for they love to stand and pray in the synagogues and on the street corners so that they may be seen by men. Truly I say to you, they have their reward in full" (Matthew 6:5.

Hypocrisy is a major theme in Jesus' teachings. In fact, he spends all of Matthew 23 cataloging the hypocrisy of the Pharisees including their pious—but powerless—prayers

Pride

It could be argued that pride, as well as the love of money, "is the root of all evil." It was Eve's pride in wanting to be like God that got the whole world in trouble. "Pride *goes* before destruction, And a haughty spirit before stumbling" (Proverbs 16:18).

God may even act to prevent pride from destroying us. The apostle Paul—some call him "Saint Paul"—had just described his spiritual revelations of meeting Jesus and being taken up to the third heaven when he wrote:

> So to keep me from becoming proud, I was given a thorn in my flesh, a messenger from Satan to torment me and keep me from becoming proud.
>
> Three different times I begged the Lord to take it away. Each time he said, "My grace is all you need. My power works best in weakness." So now I am glad to boast about my weaknesses, so that the power of Christ can work through me. That's why I take pleasure in my weaknesses, and in the insults, hardships, persecutions, and troubles that I suffer for Christ. For when I am weak, then I am strong (2 Corinthians 12:7-10 NLT).

I am grateful for ways God has not answered my grandiose—and just a bit pretentious—prayers in order to keep me from destructive pride.

Selfishness

King David writes, "Delight yourself in the Lord; And He will give you the desires of your heart" (Psalm 37:4).

At quick glance, this could imply that whatever we desire, we will get. But if we truly "delight" in the Lord, *his* desires become our desires. And because those desires are from the Lord, he will grant them.

Thomas à Kempis, in his classic devotional *The Imitation of Christ*, addresses this issue:

The Christ

    My friend, always commit your cause to me. I will bring it to fulfillment at the right time. Wait for me to orchestrate all the details, and then you will be rewarded.

The Disciple

    O Lord, freely and completely I commit all things to you, for my own planning gains me little. I wish I did not obsess on future events, but that I could offer myself completely to your pleasing will without delay.

The Christ

    My friend, often people relentlessly strive after something they desire, but when they obtain it, they have already moved on to another goal. Their desires are not lasting, and they rush on from one thing to another. So it's not really a small thing when you surrender to me in small things.[23]

When my desires line up with God's desires, there is purpose—and there are answers to prayer.

Unforgiveness

Jesus teaches, "'Whenever you stand praying, forgive, if you have anything against anyone, so that your Father who is in heaven will also forgive you your transgressions'" (Mark 11:25).

John Oglethorpe, a member of the British Parliament and founder of the colony of Georgia, boasted to John Wesley, "I never forgive." The founder of Methodism replied, "Then, sir, I hope that you never sin."

Relationships are of the utmost importance to a God who "is love" (1 John 4:7), so unforgiveness is a serious offence that can destroy our relationship with him as well as our prayer life.

Wrong motives

The apostle James, Jesus' brother, writes:

> You lust and do not have; so you commit murder. You are envious and cannot obtain; so you fight and quarrel. You do not have because you do not ask. You ask and do not receive, because you ask with wrong motives, so that you may spend it on your pleasures (James 4:2-3).

If we truly "delight in the Lord," our motives will be for the glory of the Son. They will be free from envy and selfish pleasure.

Zip, zero, zilch!

There are times that there is absolutely no wrong that we can point to that would cause God not to answer a prayer in his will.

However, here's one example of what I've dubbed "The Big Buts of the Bible." Many of the psalms begin pouting, but end in shouting:

> *But* I have trusted in Your lovingkindness; My heart shall rejoice in Your salvation. I will sing to the LORD, Because He has dealt bountifully with me (Psalm 13:5-6, *author's emphasis*).

Chelsea Rethlake, a joyful volunteer at our church and beloved teacher in public school, was an example of rejoicing in unanswered prayer. God indeed "dealt bountifully" with the twenty-four-year old. She wrote on her blog:

In October of 2011, I went from doctor to doctor and test to test in order to diagnose me with primary mediastinal lymphoma: cancer of the lymph nodes. Although having cancer is not my first choice of things to do, it's not necessarily a bad thing. I knew as soon as I was diagnosed that God could use my journey to do some incredible things. My prayer from the beginning has been that I am willing to do whatever it takes to see my family come to know the Lord, even if that means cancer.

In November 2011, I started chemo as I finished my last semester of classes and did my student teaching. It definitely wasn't easy, but the Lord is so faithful! He walked with me through every single step and placed incredible people in my life to walk beside me! The doctors were hopeful that the chemo would take care of it, but my scan showed otherwise.

In the summer of 2012, I did twenty-two radiation treatments. I was so excited about the scan following the treatment, because I was more than ready to hear my doctor tell me that I was cancer-free. Instead, I heard that the mass had actually doubled in size during radiation. Awesome. I knew I was stubborn, but I didn't know my "little pumpkin" was stubborn too. [Chelsea always jokingly referred to her tumor as her little pumpkin.]

In November 2012, I started the process of the next step in treatment: a stem cell transplant. Before I could do the transplant, though, I had to do two rounds of savage chemo to be sure it was still responsive to treatment. I've never wanted test results so badly in my life. The Lord had given me peace either way, but I just wanted to know! God proved himself faithful once more, and I had exactly 50 percent shrinkage, which is what I needed to do the process. I'm now headed to IU Cancer Center this month to do my transplant and show this cancer what's up once and for all!

Although this journey hasn't been the most pleasant experience, it has been a very blessed one. My God has revealed himself time and time again throughout the whole process. He is using me to work in people's lives that I don't even know. He has taken something that could be so ugly and nasty and made it into something beautiful. He has given me peace and joy for every step of the way when in reality there is no reason I should have felt that way. He has worked everything together for his purpose, and it has been incredible to just sit by and watch. As I begin this next step, I know without a doubt that He's got big things planned, and I'm so excited to experience them![24]

Chelsea's mother, Pam, explains those "big things."

For the past two years I have spent more time praying and wondering

> where God was in this whole ordeal. It wasn't until Chelsea was told that she had just weeks to live, that I realized what exactly was missing. It was that strong belief that God had this whole thing under control.
>
> Several weeks ago, Chels and I attended her church, both of us knowing what her situation was. Chelsea walked up to the front, started singing with her arms outstretched and a look of pure joy on her face. It was in that moment that I realized that the pure joy that was on her face was because of her amazing relationship with God and that I wanted to be able to have that same type of relationship with Him.[25]

Chelsea's prayer, "I am willing to do whatever it takes to see my family come to know the Lord, even if that means cancer" was answered in September 2013. At the standing-room-only celebration of Chelsea's short life, her mother and several relatives were baptized in recognition of their new relationship with Christ. God's purposes will be fulfilled, even if we can't see answers to our prayers.

However, during Asaph's later years, Israel's lack of answers to prayer were directly related to its willful disobedience to God's purposes. The psalmist calls the nation to repentance so that its prayers would be answered:

> *Come back, we beg you, O God of Heaven's Armies.*
> *Look down from heaven and see our plight.*
>
> *Strengthen the man you love, the son of your choice.*
> *Then we will never abandon you again.*
> *Revive us so we can call on your name once more.*
> *Turn us again to yourself, O LORD God of Heaven's Armies.*
> *Make your face shine down upon us.*
> *Only then will we be saved.*
> Psalm 80:14, 17-19 NLT

Unfulfilled Promises

5

Are God's "Promises" Really Promises?

Will the Lord reject forever?
And will He never be favorable again?
Has His lovingkindness ceased forever?
Has His promise come to an end forever?
Psalm 77:7-8

Someone has estimated that there are five thousand promises in the Bible. Many of those promises involved the rise of the Israeli kingdom.

Promises Fulfilled

During Solomon's reign, Asaph was an eyewitness to multiple fulfillments of promises:

Population growth. "Judah and Israel were as numerous as the sand that is on the seashore in abundance; they were eating and drinking and rejoicing" (1 Kings 4:20).

Widespread territory. "Solomon ruled over all the kingdoms from the River to the land of the Philistines and to the border of Egypt; they brought tribute and served Solomon all the days of his life" (1 Kings 4:21).

Peace. "For he had dominion over everything west of the River, from Tiphsah even to Gaza, over all the kings west of the River; and he had peace on all sides around about him" (1 Kings 4:24).

Kingdom prosperity. "The king made silver and gold as plentiful in Jerusalem as stone. And valuable cedar timber was as common as the sycamore-fig trees that grow in the foothills of Judah" (2 Chronicles 1:15 NLT).

Promises Unfulfilled

God's promises were being abundantly fulfilled during this time in Israel's history. But not all promises seem to be fulfilled. This was made abundantly clear when I received this heart-breaking email from a good friend who made his living writing Christian humor:

> I've been struggling with God and his promises of healing. I've had back surgery four years ago. It didn't take. My pain has increased. Like Paul, I'm trying to deal with it, but I can't anymore! So where is God and his purpose in all this? If I can't believe God for his healing, how can I trust his word for redemption/salvation? I get

angry at God. I'm frustrated with him. It affects my relationship with him!

I know many people are sick and/or hurting. How can I believe the verses about what we go through is so we can give God the glory when he's not living up to his promises? I can't witness anymore, which I'm sure makes Satan is pleased that I can't.

I'm so mad and disappointed in God![26]

Asaph struggled with those same feelings. In fact, many of the promises to the patriarchs were not yet fulfilled under Solomon's rule.

His empire was not firmly under his control. Instead of conquering and occupying lands, as God had instructed, Solomon made peace agreements with neighboring tribes and regions by marrying royalty from that group. "He had seven hundred wives, princesses, and three hundred concubines" (1 Kings 11:3a). His logic? "If I'm married to your daughter, you're less likely to attack my kingdom." At best they were one thousand peace treaties and at worst one thousand human shields.

And although his kingdom boasted four thousand stalls for his chariot horses and twelve thousand horses (1 Kings 4:26), his power was not military in nature as was his father's, David. Instead, source of power was his great wisdom: "People of all nations came to hear the wisdom of Solomon, sent by all kings of the earth, who had heard of his wisdom" (1 Kings 4:34).

Unfortunately, according to 1 Kings 11, it was Solomon's marital diplomacy that spelled the end of his rule as I shared in the Introduction.

Asaph—and all of Jerusalem—would have been aware of Solomon's idolatry through the building of the pagan shrines. And when the Temple was destroyed and Israel divided, the question of unfulfilled promises must have troubled every God-fearing Hebrew. What seemed to be a miraculous fulfillment of promises dating back to Abraham, now lay in ruins.

Our Promises Unfulfilled

Have you ever felt the way my friend, the humor writer, felt? You've seen enough of God's miracles to bolster your faith in his "promise verses," but then a loved one dies, you lose your job, the doctor pronounces a death sentence . . .

So, like Asaph, we cry out, "Has his loving kindness vanished forever? Does his promise fail for generations?" (Psalm 77:8). Sometimes it feels as if they have.

Psalm 119 makes numerous references to God's promises not being fulfilled on the author's timetable. Early Jewish scholars maintain David is the author. The language and phrasing are very Davidic, so it may refer to his conflict with his enemies—which were many. A few commentators, however, believe Psalm 119 is possibly penned by an unknown writer during Israel's exile into Babylonia. Some believe it was Ezra the prophet. Whoever the author, he is struggling with God's seeming slowness in fulfilling His promises:

> My soul languishes for Your salvation;
> I wait for Your word.
> My eyes fail *with longing* for Your word,
> While I say, "When will You comfort me?"
> Though I have become like a wineskin in the smoke,
> I do not forget Your statutes.
> How many are the days of Your servant?
> When will You execute judgment on those who persecute me?
> The arrogant have dug pits for me,
> *Men* who are not in accord with Your law.
> All Your commandments are faithful;
> They have persecuted me with a lie; help me!
> They almost destroyed me on earth,
> But as for me, I did not forsake Your precepts
> (Psalm 119:81-87).

Promises in Perspective

Does the Bible offer any clues why some promises are unfulfilled? The answer may be in more questions from the rules of biblical hermeneutics: the art and science of interpreting written text, both sacred and secular.

The apostle Paul urges us to be "Be diligent to present yourself approved to God as a workman who does not need to be ashamed, *accurately handling the word of truth* (2 Timothy 2:15, *author's emphasis*). We can do that by asking:

What was the common meaning of the word in the original language (Hebrew, Aramaic, and Greek) at the time it was written?

Words have multiple meanings. Is "blue" a color? An emotional state? A protective coating on a gun? A word to describe laws that have become obsolete but are still in force? A synonym for pornographic? The answer is "all of the above."

Not only do words have many meanings, they also change over time. Since Scripture was written over a period of sixteen hundred years—two thousand years ago—we cannot assume that the meaning of the word in, say 1600 B.C., is the same as today. Just consider how words have changed over your lifetime—or in the last year.

For instance, many modern translations render Proverbs 16:3 as "Commit your actions to the LORD, and your plans will succeed." The verse seems to promise that if we're "totally committed" to God, our plans will succeed, right? But Hebrew word translated as success, *kun*, can be translated "to be firm, be stable, be established; be enduring; to be directed aright, be fixed aright, be steadfast (moral sense); to prepare, be ready."

Success—particularly in the worldly sense of fame and fortune—is not implied. You can be firm, stable, morally steadfast and still not "succeed" on Wall Street.

The *New American Standard Bible* gets it right: "Commit your works to the LORD and your plans will be established."

Another example is the word translated "perfect" as in "Therefore you are to be perfect, as your heavenly Father is perfect" (Matthew 5:48). What? The Greek word *téleios* can also mean "complete," which seems more realistic. We can have a sense of being *complete* in God—He forgives our sins, restores our lives, promises us eternal life—without implying we can be as *perfect* as he is. "All have sinned and fall short of the glory of God" (Romans 3:23).

We certainly don't have to be Hebrew and Greek experts to discover word meanings. (I passed Greek 101 and 201 *"magna cum grace."*) Commentaries and word study books are available at most religious book stores as well as free online at BibleGateway.com, BlueLetterBible.org, and StudyLight.org.

What is the cultural context of the passage?

Take for instance Paul's prohibition against women in Ephesus teaching (1 Timothy 2:12).

First, this was likely an accommodation to the fact that women were uneducated and illiterate *during that time and place.* (It would be a bit difficult to teach when one couldn't read the Sunday school quarterly or Bible study guide!)

Secondly, some of the new converts in the church of Ephesus were former prostitutes from the temple of Diana there. These women, often recruited as young girls, knew only one way to relate to men, so some time for their spiritual maturity was essential before they took on any kind of church leadership.

Paul is not only accused by some as being sexist, but as a supporter of slavery. His command to "teach slaves to be subject to their masters in everything" (Titus 2:9 NLT) is simply acknowledging the culture of the time. Due to Roman conquests, many in the early church were slaves—and slave owners. This is why Paul commands, "Masters, grant to your slaves justice and fairness, knowing that you too have a Master in heaven" (Colossians 4:1). Paul's attitude toward the *continuance* of this practice, however, is clearly revealed in 1 Timothy 1:8-10, when he lumps slave traders in with the "lawless and rebellious . . . unholy and profane . . . those who kill their fathers or mothers . . . kidnappers . . . liars and perjurers." Not exactly a ringing endorsement for slavery! He seems to condemn further buying and selling of slaves by condemning—in no uncertain terms—slave traders.

Again, commentaries and history books can provide the cultural context of difficult passages.

Should I take everything in Scripture personally?

Many biblical "commands" do not apply to us today. For instance, the ceremonial and sacrificial laws of the Old Testament, such as circumcision, diet, Sabbath observance, etc., do not apply to Christians today. ("Thank you, Lord, we can now eat bacon!")

> [Jesus] having canceled the written code, with its regulations, that was against us and that stood opposed to us . . . took it away, nailing it to the cross . . . Therefore do not let anyone judge you by what you eat or drink, or with regard to a religious festival, a New Moon celebration or a Sabbath day. These are a shadow of the things that were to come; the reality, however, is found in [Him] (Colossians 2:14, 16-17 NLT).

The moral laws are still in force such as the Ten Commandments (Exodus 20) and "the greatest commandment" to "'love the LORD your God with all your heart, all your soul, all your mind, and all your strength.' The second is equally important: 'Love your neighbor as yourself.' No other commandment is greater than these" (Mark 12:30-31 quoting Leviticus 19:18).

We need to be careful to understand who the author is in confusing passages. For instance, what should we do with this verse? "A feast is made for laughter, and wine makes life merry, but money is the answer for everything" (Ecclesiastes 10:19 NIV). I do not recommend it for your "life verse." The book is a "journal" written by a man exploring the meaning of life through wine, women, and riches. He eventually comes to the right conclusion that all those things are "vane." And, if as some think, Solomon wrote the book, this philosophy did *not* end well.

This is why it's so important to ask:

What is the broadest, most documented position?

Lee Haines, one of my college professors, suggested we avoid Bible study tools to look up "proof texts."

"If you have to look through the entire Bible each time you want to prove something, you'll see what *God* has to say, not just some verse to prove what *you* want to say." He's right. With over twenty-three thousand verses from which to choose, we can find a verse to prove our point on almost any subject.

This overview is important when it comes to the two specific prohibitions against women in leadership (1 Corinthians 14:34-36, 1 Timothy 2:12). In contrast to these two isolated passages, there are hundreds of verses describing godly women in administrative and teaching roles: Miriam (prophet—there is *no* distinction between "prophets" and "prophetess" in Hebrew scripture), Deborah (prophet, judge, military leader), Hulda (prophet), Noadiah (prophet), Anna (prophet), Mary Magdalene, Joanna, Susanna and "many others" (Christ's disciples), Mary Magdalene (the first evangelist), the daughters of Philip (prophets), Priscilla (teacher), Chloe (house church leader), Mary the mother of John (house church leader), Lydia (house church leader), Nympha of Laodicea (house church leader), and Phoebe (deacon, *not* "deaconess" as translated in the KJV).

David Thompson, Hebrew and Greek scholar from Asbury Seminary, notes, "Do we read the entire Bible in light of these two problematic texts, or do we read these two texts in light of the entire Bible?"

Does the "biblical commandment" square with "the greatest commandment"?

Paul notes in Romans 13:8-10:
> Owe nothing to anyone—except for your obligation to love one another. If you love your neighbor, you will fulfill the requirements of God's law. For the commandments say, "You must not commit adultery. You must not

murder. You must not steal. You must not covet." These—and other such commandments—are summed up in this one commandment: "Love your neighbor as yourself." Love does no wrong to others, so love fulfills the requirements of God's law.

I believe carefully analyzing Scripture—and specifically examining biblical promises—does not show disrespect to God's Word, but exhibits an even higher level of respect. I want to know *accurately* what God wanted to convey to his followers—and to me.

Is the Promise for You and Me?

I had a pastor friend who never prepared for his sermons. Not even Saturday night. His rationale: "Take ye no thought how or what thing ye shall answer, or what ye shall say. For the Holy Ghost shall teach you in the same hour what ye ought to say" (Luke 12:11-12 KJV).

He accused me of not trusting the Holy Spirit and studying too much "in the flesh" as I prepped for talks at conferences. (I must confess, I *am* a "Doomsday Prepper" when it comes to keynote talks.)

However, there's only one problem with using that as a promise for not having to study. It applies to those who are being hauled into court to defend their faith—not before the congregation on Sunday morning.

> *"When they bring you before the synagogues, the rulers, and the authorities,* don't be anxious how or what you will answer, or what you will say; for the Holy Spirit will teach you in that same hour what you must say" (Luke 12:11-12, *author's emphasis*).

This is the problem of pulling "promise verses" out of context. Is this a specific promise to a specific person? Is it a promise for a certain time in God's timeline? Or is it a universal promise for all believers for all time?

Is the promise conditional?

Many biblical promises are if/then propositions. *If* you do this, *then* God will do that. For instance, this is pretty straightforward: "If they [do what is just and right], then they will surely live and not die" (Ezekiel 33:15 NLT).

We'll talk more about this in the next chapter. For now, remember some promises are conditioned on our actions and attitudes. God will not act upon the promise until we have fulfilled our part of the agreement.

And it's important to note that freewill also plays an important part in the fulfillment. I have talked with so many parents who are heartbroken by the apparent lack of fulfillment of this promise: "Direct your children onto the right path, and when they are older, they will not leave it" (Proverbs 22:6 NLT).

Mr. and Mrs. Manoah were model parents. Living in a land that "did evil in the eyes of the Lord," they ate a kosher diet, prayed to the one true God, offered sacrifices, and didn't even drink. A Jewish mother would have been proud to have them for a son and daughter-in-law. And after being childless for years, an angel of the Lord announced they would have a son. What joy as he "grew and the Lord blessed him, and the Spirit of the Lord began to stir him." The son of these godly parents was none other than—Samson, Israel's playboy strong man who lost his hair and God-given power to Delilah's deadly charms.

Two friends of mine raised their children in a Christian home, complete with family devotions, and regular church attendance, and leadership. (All names have been changed.) Their daughter, Janet, became involved in drinking and drugs while living in a homosexual relationship. The other daughter, Marie, also used alcohol and drugs while living with her boyfriend. Their son Ross also abused alcohol and drugs.

It was heart-breaking to hear my friends beat up themselves for not being "better parents." I tried to encourage them, while parents can model their faith and fervently pray for their children, their offspring still have a free-will. Even God, who obviously is the godliest parent, doesn't have a perfect record as far as children go. His first two—Adam and Eve—rebelled even though he gave them his undivided attention. And the nation of Israel was a rebellious, ungrateful child. So, the Father knows the heart of the parent with a prodigal child.

It is encouraging to note that Samson did come back to God. And that now that "they are older," Marie and her boyfriend are now husband and wife serving as Christian missionaries. Ross came to Christ and is working in social services. It broke her parents' heart when Janet married her female lover—but her story is not over yet—and neither are the stories of countless prodigal children.

Is the promise in context?

Many of our favorite "promise verses" may not promise what we think they promise.

For instance, Philippians 4:13 promises, "I can do all this through him who gives me strength." This verse has been passionately applied to everything from passing a college class to raising funds for a church building project to kicking a bad habit.

But look at it in context:

> But I rejoiced in the Lord greatly, that now at last you have revived your concern for me; indeed, you were concerned *before*, but you lacked opportunity. Not that I speak from want, for *I have learned to be content in whatever circumstances I am.* I know how to get along with humble means, and I also know how to live in prosperity; in any and every circumstance I have learned the secret of being filled and going hungry, both

> of having abundance and suffering need. I can do all things through Him who strengthens me (Philippians 4:10-13, *author's emphasis*).

What Paul can "do" through the Lord is to live with *contentment*. Another snippet of a verse promises all manner of blessings:

> "Give, and it will be given to you. They will pour into your lap a good measure—pressed down, shaken together, and running over. For by your standard of measure it will be measured to you in return" (Luke 6:38).

I'm sure you've heard this verse as the basis for generous financial giving. But look at the verse preceding it to find out just *what* is being given: "Do not judge, and you will not be judged; and do not condemn, and you will not be condemned; pardon, and you will be pardoned" (6:37 NLT). Forgiveness—not financial gain—is promised; mercy—not money.

Another out-of-context promise allegedly promises "good gifts."

> "Now suppose one of you fathers is asked by his son for a fish; he will not give him a snake instead of a fish, will he? Or if he is asked for an egg, he will not give him a scorpion, will he?" (Luke 11:11).

I have heard that verse completely wrenched out of context. Well-meaning readers assume that this means nothing bad will happen to believers—only wonderful gifts. And when they pull back the wrapping paper and find stones and scorpions, they become upset and angry at God believing him to be the giver. However, it's important to know what gift is actually promised.

> If you then, being evil, know how to give good gifts to your children, how much more will your heavenly Father give the Holy Spirit to those who ask Him?" (Luke 11:12-13).

No, it is not material or temporal gain. It's *the Holy Spirit*. And I am more than abundantly blessed with God's presence that has given me hope and humor through times it would have been easier to mope and murmur. God's Spirit is infinitely more valuable than anything we could think or imagine.

In my study of Scripture, I've found that the majority of God's promises—read in context—are for our spiritual maturity—not material gain. Peter writes to the early church that is facing severe persecution. If any time is a good time for promises, it was then. But notice what kinds of things are promised:

> [His] divine power has granted to us everything pertaining to life and godliness, through the true knowledge of Him who called us by His own glory and excellence. For by these He has granted to us His precious and magnificent promises, so that by them you may become partakers of the divine nature, having escaped the corruption that is in the world by lust. Now for this very reason also, applying all *diligence*, in your *faith* supply moral *excellence*, and in your moral excellence, *knowledge*, and in your knowledge, *self-control*, and in your self-control, *perseverance*, and in your perseverance, *godliness*, and in your godliness, *brotherly kindness*, and in your brotherly kindness, *love*. For if these qualities are yours and are increasing, they render

> you neither useless nor unfruitful in the true knowledge of our Lord Jesus Christ (2 Peter 1:3-8, *author's emphasis*).

Finally, some "promises" are not even in the Bible. You won't find, "God helps those who help themselves" in the Bible. And you definitely won't find, "God will not give you more than you can bear." So, when professing Christians, in utter desperation, attempt to take their own lives, many believers piously assume that these troubled people weren't Christian at all. That so-called promise—not more than we can bear—is not in the Bible but is twisted out of context from 1 Corinthians 10:13:

> The temptations in your life are no different from what others experience. And God is faithful. He will not allow the temptation to be more than you can stand. When you are tempted, he will show you a way out so that you can endure.

It's about *temptation*, not about the heavy weight of life. I've met too many saintly Christians tormented because of an overwhelming physical or mental issue that they cannot bear—that has nothing to do with "temptation." And yet others misuse this "promise verse" to add to the pain because they aren't handling life well.

Is the promise for today?

Many believers consider Jeremiah 29:11 their "life verse." "For I know the plans I have for you," says the Lord. "They are plans for good and not for disaster, to give you a future and a hope" (NLT).

It looks very comforting on a plaque at the Christian book store, however, look at the verses *before* and *after*:

> For thus says the Lord. "When seventy years have been completed for Babylon,

> I will visit you and fulfill My good word to you, to bring you back to this place. For I know the plans that I have for you," declares the LORD, "plans for welfare and not for calamity to give you a future and a hope. Then you will call upon Me and come and pray to Me, and I will listen to you" (Jeremiah 29:10-12).

God's "plans" are to discipline the Israeli people with *seventy years of captivity*.

Wilbur Williams, professor of Old Testament at Indiana Wesleyan University, believes that many promises and prophesies are brought into being through a growing spiral of fulfillment. While the promises for the Jewish kingdom were partially fulfilled under King Solomon, they will be fully fulfilled in Christ's Kingdom.

For instance, many of the promises given to the ancient patriarchs of Israel have yet to be fulfilled. In Genesis 13, God makes the following promises:

> On that day the LORD made a covenant with Abram, saying,
>
> "To your descendants I have given this land, From the river of Egypt as far as the great river, the river Euphrates: the Kenite and the Kenizzite and the Kadmonite and the Hittite and the Perizzite and the Rephaim and the Amorite and the Canaanite and the Girgashite and the Jebusite" (Genesis 15:18-21).

The vast stretch of real estate promised to Abraham reaches from the Nile to the Euphrates Rivers including the eastern portion of Egypt, including the Sinai Peninsula, modern day Israel, Jordan, Lebanon, the western two-thirds of Syria, the western half of Iraq, and northern portions of Saudi Arabia and Kuwait.

Under Joshua, Israel conquered only a fraction of that promised land. "Now Joshua was old *and* advanced in years when the LORD said to him, 'You are old *and* advanced in years, and very much of the land remains to be possessed'" (13:1). Very much land!

Judges 1 provides a list of tribes in the promised territory that the Israelites failed to conquer. They did force the Canaanites and Amorites to work as slaves but never completely drove them out of the land (1:28, 1:36).

Solomon, following David's military exploits, extended Israel's sphere of influence so that he could demand tributes from between the rivers (1 Kings 4:21). However, Israel—in disobedience—never truly occupied the land, so God's promise to Abraham that his descendants would *possess* the land between the rivers has never been truly fulfilled.

But there is a day coming when the Son of David will rule over the entire world. Dr. William's concept of spiraling fulfillment will expand to God's ultimate fulfillment.

> For a child will be born to us, a son will be given to us; And the government will rest on His shoulders; And His name will be called Wonderful Counselor, Mighty God, Eternal Father, Prince of Peace. There will be no end to the increase of *His* government or of peace, On the throne of David and over his kingdom, To establish it and to uphold it with justice and righteousness From then on and forevermore. The zeal of the LORD of hosts will accomplish this (Isaiah 9:6-7).

Paul picks up on Christ as the fulfillment of the ancient promise to Abraham:

> What's more, the Scriptures looked forward to this time when God would make the Gentiles right in his sight

> because of their faith. God proclaimed this good news to Abraham long ago when he said, "All nations will be blessed through you." So all who put their faith in Christ share the same blessing Abraham received because of his faith (Galatians 3:8-9).

Gentiles, non-Jewish people, are now a part of the promise God made four thousand years ago to Abraham: "And through your descendants all the nations of the earth will be blessed—all because you have obeyed me" (Genesis 22:18).

Followers of Christ—the children of Abraham—do indeed fill the earth on every continent and every country. And in the last days, "All nations will come and worship before you, for your righteous deeds have been revealed" (Revelation 15:4b).

Finally, the apostle Peter provides some answers to the slowness of God fulfillment of promises:

> But do not let this one fact escape your notice, beloved, that with the Lord one day is like a thousand years, and a thousand years like one day. The Lord is not slow about His promise, as some count slowness, but is patient toward you, not wishing for any to perish but for all to come to repentance (2 Peter 3:8-9, *author's emphasis*).

If God was not "slow concerning his promise" and returned soon after his ascension into heaven, you and I would never have had the chance to be born and spend eternity with him. But first, we must wait—with our questions.

I love Asaph's transparency and vulnerability as he waited for answers to prayer, the punishment of evil, and the fulfillment of promises. This was a man entrusted with the musical praise of God's people. Yet he honestly poured out his questions and confusion: "Has

His lovingkindness ceased forever? Has his promise come to an end forever?" (Psalm 77:8). Yet, in the very next psalm, he writes:

O my people, listen to my instructions.
Open your ears to what I am saying,
for I will speak to you in a parable.
I will teach you hidden lessons from our past—
stories we have heard and known,
stories our ancestors handed down to us.
We will not hide these truths from our children;
we will tell the next generation
about the glorious deeds of the LORD,
about his power and his mighty wonders.

So each generation should set its hope anew on God,
not forgetting his glorious miracles
and obeying his commands.
Psalm 78:1-4, 7 NLT

6

Are the Promises Conditional?

*And they remembered that God was their rock,
And the Most High God their Redeemer.
But they deceived Him with their mouth
And lied to Him with their tongue.
For their heart was not steadfast toward Him,
Nor were they faithful in His covenant.*

*But He, being compassionate, forgave their iniquity
and did not destroy them;
And often He restrained His anger
And did not arouse all His wrath.*

> *How often they rebelled against Him in the wilderness*
> *And grieved Him in the desert!*
> *Again and again they tempted God,*
> *And pained the Holy One of Israel.*
> *They did not remember His power,*
> *The day when He redeemed them from the adversary. . . .*
> *Psalm 78:35-38, 41-42*

God's promises are often *quid pro quo* propositions. The Latin phrase means "something for something." In legal terms it's a contract: "If the party of the first part does this, then the party of the second part must do that." The best-known verse in the Bible, John 3:16, is an if/then proposition. "For God so loved the world that He gave His only begotten Son, that whoever believes in Him shall not perish, but have eternal life."

If you believe in God's own Son, *then* you will not perish but have eternal life.

In fact, the entire Bible—from Genesis to Revelation—is based on if/then propositions.

> You will be accepted if you do what is right. But if you refuse to do what is right, then watch out! Sin is crouching at the door, eager to control you. But you must subdue it and be its master (Genesis 4:7 NLT).

> "For if you forgive others for their transgressions, your heavenly Father will also forgive you. But if you do not forgive others, then your Father will not forgive your transgressions" (Matthew 6:14-15).

> If you confess with your mouth Jesus as Lord, and believe in your heart that God raised Him from the dead, you will be saved (Romans 10:9).

"If you remain faithful even when facing death, I will give you the crown of life" (Revelation 2:10c).

"Behold, I stand at the door and knock; if anyone hears My voice and opens the door, I will come in to him and will dine with him, and he with Me" (Revelation 3:20).

Notice the if/then propositions promised to Solomon as he began his reign:

If . . .

"[you] keep the charge of the LORD your God, to walk in His ways, to keep His statutes, His commandments, His ordinances, and His testimonies, according to what is written in the Law of Moses . . ." (1 Kings 2:3)

". . . your sons are careful of their way, to walk before Me in truth with all their heart and with all their soul . . ." (1 Kings 2:4)

". . . you will walk in My statutes and execute My ordinances and keep all My commandments by walking in them . . ." (1 Kings 6:12).

Then . . .

". . . you may succeed in all that you do and wherever you turn" (1 Kings 2:3).

" . . . you shall not lack a man on the throne of Israel" (1 Kings 2:4).

> "... I will carry out My word with you which I spoke to David your father. I will dwell among the sons of Israel, and will not forsake My people Israel" (1 Kings 6:12-13)

Sadly, Solomon and his sons did not fulfill the if/then covenant with God—and the kingdom collapsed under the weight of idolatry and greed.

So, yes, many biblical promises require us to do something—or more important *be* something—before God will act.

Dallas Willard, in *The Great Omission: Reclaiming Jesus' Essential Teaching on Discipleship*, cautions that this is not the same as "salvation" by works. "Grace is not opposed to effort, it is opposed to earning. Earning is an attitude. Effort is an action. Grace, you know, does not just have to do with forgiveness of sins alone."

Jesus provides if/then propositions for and beyond salvation:

> "I am the vine; you are the branches. If a man remains in me and I in him, he will bear much fruit; apart from me you can do nothing. If anyone does not remain in me, [then] he is like a branch that is thrown away and withers; such branches are picked up, thrown into the fire and burned" (John 15:1-6 NLT).

This has nothing to do with "works." It is simply the natural, organic outflow of the branch (us) being connected to the vine (Jesus)—as natural as apple trees producing apples.

However, the question rears up when follow all the *ifs*, but God is not fulfilling his *then* promise. Which brings us to the next chapter.

> *"Call upon Me in the day of trouble;*
> *I shall rescue you, and you will honor Me."*
> Psalm 50:15

7

Are the Promises to Be Fulfilled in the Future?

When I pondered to understand [the prosperity of the wicked],
It was troublesome in my sight
Until I came into the sanctuary of God;
Then I perceived their end.
Surely You set them in slippery places;
You cast them down to destruction.
How they are destroyed in a moment!
They are utterly swept away by sudden terrors!
Like a dream when one awakes,
O Lord, when aroused, You will despise their form.
Psalm 73:16-20

Asaph had witnessed the long and winding road which led to the Ark being returned to Jerusalem, the first permanent Temple erected to the establishment of a peaceful kingdom—just as God had promised. While the rise of David as king until his son Solomon completed the Temple are only a few chapters in Scripture, there were many years of waiting. A fifteen-year wait between David anointed as king and crowned king of Judah. Then seven and a half years after that, until he became king of all of Israel. He ruled for forty years, while the Israelites worshiped God in a tent. It took seven years to complete the Temple under Solomon.

It seems the Israelites spent most of their time waiting. Forty-three times, in the Old Testament alone, God commands his people to wait.

There is a thirty-year wait between God's promise to Abraham for a son. A four-hundred to four-hundred-and thirty-year wait enslaved in Egypt, including Moses' forty years tending sheep in the desert to set his people free. The Israelites waited forty years wandering in the wilderness—as a consequence of their rebellion and disobedience—before they reached the Promised Land.

Earlier, I wrote about the promise of Jeremiah 29:11. Remember, this was promised *before* seventy years of waiting in captivity in Babylon.

Then a four-hundred-year wait between the Old and New Testaments in which God was completely silent.

Even the last words in the New Testament are about waiting: "Behold, I am coming quickly, and My reward *is* with Me, to render to every man according to what he has done (Revelation 22:12). That "quick" return has taken nearly two thousand years now.

Part of our frustration is that we are locked in time—and God isn't. As the familiar verse notes: "But do not let this one *fact* escape your notice, beloved, that with the Lord one day is like a thousand years, and a thousand years like one day" (2 Peter 3:8).

In Chapter 1 we looked at reasons why God delays answers to prayers. In this chapter, let's look at how we can respond to waiting for promises. But first, let's be clear. Waiting is no fun, whether you're a kid waiting for Christmas, a single young person waiting for a spouse, or an adult waiting for test results.

The Bible provides some attitudes to exhibit during the "wait" of living.

Confidently

The author of Hebrews writes, "Now faith is the assurance of things hoped for, the conviction of things not seen" (Hebrews 11:1).

The word translated "assurance" in Greek is *hypostasis*. In English, hypostasis is "an underlying reality or substance, as opposed to attributes or that which lacks substance." Joseph Henry Thayer, a noted New Testament Greek scholar, defines it as "a foundation which is firm . . . real . . . substantial quality." It is as solid and steady as God.

The apostle Paul writes, "But if we look forward to something we don't yet have, we must wait patiently and confidently" (Romans 8:25 NLT).

Hopefully

I've described H.O.P.E. as Holding On for a Positive Ending. "And the Scriptures give us hope and encouragement as we wait patiently for God's promises to be fulfilled" (Romans 15:4 NLT).

George Matheson describes the struggle of hope delayed:

> There are times when things look very dark to me—so dark that I have to wait even for hope. It is bad enough to wait *in* hope. A long-deferred fulfillment carries its own pain, but to wait *for* hope, to see no glimmer of a prospect and yet refuse to despair; to have nothing but night before the casement and yet to keep the casement open for possible stars; to have a vacant place in my heart and yet to allow that place to be filled by no inferior presence—that is the grandest patience in the universe. It is Job in the tempest; it is Abraham on the road to Moriah; it is Moses in the desert of Midian; it is the Son of man in the Garden of Gethsemane.

> I shall reach the climax of strength
> when I have learned to wait for hope.[27]

Memorably

Asaph was in "deep trouble" and describes his agony in Psalm 77. But notice, right in the middle he makes a sudden U-turn as he remembers God's "wonderful deeds of long ago." Buckle your seatbelt!

> My voice *rises* to God, and I will cry aloud; My voice *rises* to God, and He will hear me.
>
> In the day of my trouble I sought the Lord; In the night my hand was stretched out without weariness; My soul refused to be comforted.
>
> *When* I remember God, then I am disturbed; *When* I sigh, then my spirit grows faint. You have held my eyelids *open*; I am so troubled that I cannot speak
>
> I have considered the days of old, The years of long ago. I will remember my song in the night; I will meditate with my heart, And my spirit ponders:
>
> Will the Lord reject forever? And will He never be favorable again? Has His lovingkindness ceased forever? Has *His* promise come to an end forever?
>
> Has God forgotten to be gracious, Or has He in anger withdrawn His compassion?

> Then I said, "It is my grief, That the right hand of the Most High has changed" (77:1-10)

[Sound of tires squealing!]

> I shall remember the deeds of the LORD; Surely I will remember Your wonders of old. I will meditate on all Your work And muse on Your deeds. Your way, O God, is holy; What god is great like our God? You are the God who works wonders; You have made known Your strength among the peoples. You have by Your power redeemed Your people, The sons of Jacob and Joseph.
>
> You led Your people like a flock By the hand of Moses and Aaron (77:11-15).

By thanking God for what he has done in the past, we have confidence he will do the same in the future. I remember a truly memorable provision:

For two years in the late 70s, my wife and I traveled the United States in a motor home conducting "Kid's Krusades," youth programs, and adult Bible teaching seminars. While on our way to services in Pennsylvania, 'Arvey—our RV—began growling and then coasted to a sickening stop just beyond a gate on the Ohio Turnpike. We were towed to Al's Transmission Shop in a tiny town with no hotel, so for two days we lived in the broken-down RV in the repair bay. Early in the morning, we would feel our home rising to a 45° angle as they worked at rebuilding the transmission. Then we were lowered at night.

While writing checks for bills at that angle, we really struggled with the question, "Do we pay the Lord or Al?" We decided to mail our tithe to our church and pay the bill with a credit card. The bill was five *hundred* dollars, which at that time was about a month's net income. "God, help!" When we arrived at our denominational headquarters to pick up our mail, we found an envelope from one of my parents' friends. She had appreciated our ministry and enclosed a check—for five *thousand* dollars! God certainly honored our obedience in paying our tithe!

When I am discouraged, I look back at my journals and discover hundreds of "wonderful deeds of long ago" when God has abundantly provided.

However, giving our tithes is not a *quid pro quo* investment scheme. We have not always seen such dramatic provisions, but our daily needs have been faithfully provided.

Patiently

Patience and waiting also seem to go together like love and marriage. King David writes, "I waited patiently for the Lord; And He inclined to me and heard my cry (Psalm 40:1).

I still struggle with waiting patiently. The day before I would learn if the radiation had destroyed the prostate cancer I posted online:

> I still haven't mastered waiting!
>
> A year of waiting for multiple PSA results, all a bit higher than the last. Waiting for a biopsy. Waiting for the biopsy results. Waiting for treatment to begin once the doctor dropped the C-bomb. Waiting for the final results. I had my last "zap" August 28 and will finally get results tomorrow [October 14].
>
> And then waiting one to two years to see if the radiation will cause incontinence or impotence.
>
> I'll post the results of the treatment as soon as I know them, so thanks for

> waiting with me and especially your prayers. I don't do waiting well, but I have felt a miraculous peace during this time. And for that, I am grateful—and amazed.

I really did feel peace as I sat in the waiting room waiting to learn the life-and-death news. Thankfully, good news that day—and two years later!

Persistently

In Galatians 6:9, the apostle Paul encourages us: "Let us not lose heart in doing good, for in due time we will reap if we do not grow weary."

While I may not be patient, I am persistent—or perhaps bullheaded. But persistence needs to be balanced with patience. And I have learned that waiting is much braver and more courageous that blindly plowing ahead.

Quietly

I love Moses' instructions as the fleeing Israelites were between a rock and a hard place. Actually two hard places: the Egyptian army and the Red Sea.

> Moses said to the people, "Do not fear! Stand by and see the salvation of the LORD which He will accomplish for you today; for the Egyptians whom you have seen today, you will never see them again forever. The LORD will fight for you *while you keep silent*" (Exodus 14:13-14, *author's emphasis*).

As I've written this book, I've continually asked myself, *Should I share this?* I want this book to be real, honest, and transparent. No sugar coating. But I'm grateful for first readers and godly editors who have advised, "Maybe that's something for a trusted friend or a safe small group—or a therapist! It may be best to follow Moses' admonition and 'keep silent.' The Lord will fight for you.'"

I do believe that honestly sharing our struggles is important—thus this book—but we need to ask, "Will this be helpful to my readers, our Facebook friends, small group, co-workers, etc.? Or will it stir up unnecessary questions and doubts?" Asaph struggled with this as well:

> Did I keep my heart pure for nothing? Did I keep myself innocent for no reason? I get nothing but trouble all day long; every morning brings me pain. If I had really spoken this way to others, I would have been a traitor to your people (Psalm 73:13-15 NLT).

Remember C. S. Lewis' disheartening description of God's silence as "a door slammed in your face, and a sound of bolting and double bolting on the inside." That was originally written as a personal letter that I suspect was never intended for the public.

Later, when he's had a chance to think it through for publication, he writes in *A Grief Observed*:

> I have gradually been coming to feel that the door is no longer shut and bolted. Was it my own frantic need that slammed it in my face? The time when there is nothing at all in your soul except a cry for help may be just the time when God can't give it: you are like the drowning man who can't be helped because he clutches and grabs. Perhaps your own reiterated cries deafen you to the voice you hoped to hear.[28]

Thankfully

I love the attitude of Habakkuk,

> Though the fig tree should not blossom And there be no fruit on the vines, *Though* the yield of the olive should fail And the fields produce no food, Though the flock should be cut off from the fold And there be no cattle in the stalls, Yet I will exult in the Lord, I will rejoice in the God of my salvation (Habakkuk 3:17-18).

Little is known of the prophet Habakkuk except that he lived in the time when Israel was oppressed and many had been taken captive by the Babylonians. There was little reason to give thanks. Maybe you feel you have little for which to give thanks.

Despite living in captivity—along with Daniel and Jeremiah—and facing what appears to be a famine, Habakkuk writes, "Yet, I will rejoice in the Lord!"

Things were no better six hundred years later when the apostle Paul wrote during a time of another political oppression. Israel was occupied by Rome and the infamous Nero had just been appointed to rule over God's promised land. So, Paul also had little reason for which to give thanks, yet he writes, "in everything give thanks; for this is God's will for you in Christ Jesus" (1 Thessalonians 5:18).

Notice that Habakkuk and Paul are not giving thanks *for* their situations, but *in* their situations. And the author of Hebrews encourages Christ followers to offer a "sacrifice of praise" (13:14), even though he is writing in the context of bearing the "disgrace" Jesus bore (13:13).

One morning I woke up feeling depressed and despondent. I decided to make a list of things for which I could give thanks. I found fifty things just between the bed and bathroom:

1. God's protection and providence (I woke up!)
2. His love and grace
3. I slept straight through the night
4. No horrible nightmares resulting from real-life trauma
5. I don't work the night shift

6. My CPAP (Constant Positive Air Pressure) machine, which keeps me breathing at night, was a gift.
7. I woke up refreshed
8. I can hear the cell phone alarm
9. Cell phones
10. Electricity
11. Birds singing
12. I can see the cell phone
13. I can click "snooze"
14. I have two working hands and arms
15. I can get out of bed on my own
16. Or, I can pull up the covers and roll over
17. I'm not in pain
18. Clean air
19. I'm waking up in a warm water bed with flannel sheets [It was January.]
20. I'm waking up in a warm, dry house with new furnace and central air
21. The house isn't in foreclosure
22. I'm waking up in a free country
23. I'm not waking up in a war-torn country
24. I'm not waking up in prison
25. I'm not waking up in a hospital
26. I'm not waking up in a nursing home
27. I can walk unassisted: no crutches, walkers, braces or casts

[Walking past closet]

28. Lots of clothes in the closet—and on the floor
29. Walking on wall-to-wall carpeting rather than dirt
30. Sense of touch: toes on carpeting

[Walking past photos of kids and grandkids]

31. Loving family
32. Loving, faithful Christian wife
33. Both kids are gainfully employed in serving others
34. Both kids are strong Christians
35. Grandkiddos!
36. And all five grandkiddos are indeed *grand*.
37. The picture of daughter at seven with mischievous grin always makes me smile

[Walking past office]

38. Being able to work from home since 1982
39. Hundreds of advantages of being self-employed such as being there for wife, kids, and grandkids in good and bad times
40. Computers: A love/hate relationship, but I wouldn't be a writer if I had to do all that re-typing!
41. Laptop and desk
42. The Internet, email, Facebook
43. Meaningful service for God
44. Meaningful work—at least today
45. Remembering where the bathroom is. No Alzheimer's—yet.
46. The house has indoor plumbing
47. My "plumbing" is working fine after successful radiation for cancer!
48. I can read
49. Freedom of the press
50. Toilet paper

And most of all, the promise of God's presence to be with me, no matter what I face today, tomorrow—and eternally. However, the promised fulfillment doesn't always come in this life!

Hebrews 11 is known as the "Faith Chapter." Verse after verse, celebrating Bible characters . . .

> . . . who by faith conquered kingdoms, performed *acts of* righteousness, obtained promises, shut the mouths of lions, quenched the power of fire, escaped the edge of the sword, from weakness were made strong, became mighty in war, put foreign armies to flight. Women received *back* their dead by resurrection . . . (11:33-35a).

But without even a sentence break, it continues:

> . . . and others were tortured, not accepting their release, so that they might obtain a better resurrection Others experienced mockings and scourgings, yes, also chains and imprisonment. They were stoned, they were sawn in two, they were tempted, they were put to death with the sword; they went about in sheepskins, in goatskins, being destitute, afflicted, ill-treated (*men* of whom the world was not worthy), wandering in deserts and mountains and caves and holes in the ground. And all these, having gained approval through their faith, did not receive what was promised, because God had provided something better for us, so that apart from us they would not be made perfect (11:35b-40).

I love the truthfulness of the Bible. Sometimes God's promises are not fulfilled here and now. God has promised—and provided—something infinitely "better" and "perfect." In the time it's taken me to write this book, three godly friends have died of cancer. They were not healed here and now, but I have no doubt they are in eternity.

So, I will wait—hopefully patiently—until God makes everything "perfect."

Do not deliver the soul of Your turtledove to the wild beast;
Do not forget the life of Your afflicted forever.
Consider the covenant;
For the dark places of the land are full of the habitations of violence.
Let not the oppressed return dishonored;
Let the afflicted and needy praise Your name.
Arise, O God, and plead Your own cause. . . .
Psalm 74:19-22a

Unpunished Evil

8

Is God Responsible for Evil?

O God, why have you rejected us so long?
Why is your anger so intense against the sheep of your own pasture?
Remember that we are the people you chose long ago,
the tribe you redeemed as your own special possession!
And remember Jerusalem, your home here on earth.
Walk through the awful ruins of the city;
see how the enemy has destroyed your sanctuary.

We no longer see your miraculous signs.
All the prophets are gone,
and no one can tell us when it will end.

> *How long, O God, will you allow our enemies to insult you?*
> *Will you let them dishonor your name forever?*
> Psalm 74:1-3, 9-10 NLT

Asaph's lament sums up other biblical authors who struggled with questions of unpunished evil throughout Scripture (Ecclesiastes 3:16, Ecclesiastes 4:1, Proverbs 36:12, Jeremiah 12:1, Habakkuk 1:2-4). But throughout Scripture, we see this truth:

God Loves Righteousness and Justice

Despite our struggles with unpunished evil—from Genesis through Revelation—God is portrayed as a righteous God. Because of that nature, he desires justice. In fact, righteousness and justice also appear throughout Scripture as conjoined twins that cannot be separated.

> He loves righteousness and justice;
> The earth is full of the lovingkindness
> of the Lord (Psalm 33:5).

> Your righteousness is like the mighty mountains, your justice like the ocean depths. You care for people and animals alike, O Lord (Psalm 36:6 NLT).

> Righteousness and justice are the foundation of your throne. Unfailing love and truth walk before you as attendants (Psalm 89:14 NLT).

Because God's character is infinite holiness, he cannot be or condone anything that is not righteous and just. No sooner had I posted that concept on Facebook, I received this response:

> Actually, evil was "created" by God (Isaiah 45:7) before He created any

> beings. Because He is love and love does not demand its own way, God withdrew Himself from a "place" to give a choice to His created beings. After Lucifer/Satan chose to let go of God and to set up his own kingdom in the alternative to God, our Father went to that place and created our world.

I had to respectfully disagree with her.

First, God's character is absolute holiness (Exodus 15:11, 1 Samuel 2:2) and love (1 John 4:7) and because of that character he can never create evil. Everything in Creation was called good. The creation of man and woman was declared "very good."

Second, evil itself cannot be created. Darkness was not created; it is the absence of light. You cannot create darkness, and all the darkness in the world cannot extinguish light. To be more simplistic, there's no such thing as a hole—it's simply the absence of dirt or donut dough. There's no such thing as a "dark bulb."

Evil is a choice. It is only demonstrated by God's creations (angelic and human) because of a willful choice. (God did create "freewill" but not evil. That's a whole other discussion.) Because God's character only chooses good, He cannot demonstrate evil. He is love and thus every action is holy, pure, and good.

James places the responsibility for evil squarely on his creations: "And remember, when you are being tempted, do not say, 'God is tempting me.' God is never tempted to do wrong, and he never tempts anyone else. Temptation comes from our own desires, which entice us and drag us away. These desires give birth to sinful actions. And when sin is allowed to grow, it gives birth to death" (James 1:13-15).

Third, the context of Isaiah 45:7 is that God creates good and bad times to accomplish his will. Verse 24 notes that despite what evil

Israel's enemies will bring against them, Israel ". . . will say of me, 'In the LORD alone are deliverance and strength.'"

I hope that's helpful. Bottom line, one verse out of context does not contradict the truth that God is absolute holiness and love and thus cannot, because of his perfect character, create or do evil.

We find in the rule of David and Solomon, brief moments in Israel's history where justice and righteousness prevailed: "So David reigned over all Israel; and David administered justice and righteousness for all his people" (2 Samuel 8:15).
However . . .

People Abuse God's Freewill

One of the most wonderful and frightening gifts God created is freewill. All his creatures are motivated by instincts, stimulus/response, and their "lizard brains"—except human beings. As creatures created in the "image of God," we possess freewill to make choices, and we can anticipate the consequences of those choices. (Humans can choose to make decisions above and beyond what simply feels good.) And, as the only creatures who can communicate in words and symbols, we are hardwired for relationships.

God is all about relationships. In fact, 1 John 4:7 declares "God is love." But for love to be reciprocal—two-sided—it must be voluntary. There must be a choice to either love or reject the love.

God "rejoices" over those who choose to love him. Isn't that an amazing concept? But it is only possible with our being free to make that choice.

However, there is great debate in all religions on the limits of freewill. In Christianity, Calvinists stress the sovereignty of God. We see this in Romans 9, where souls are described as clay in God's hands. Wesleyan-Arminians stress freewill. Romans 10 stresses our choices in salvation.

I tend to put this sovereignty/freewill issue in the same "Things I Don't Understand" file as other conundrums such as "God is three-in-one" and "Jesus is both God and Man."

If pressed, I would have to describe myself as a "Cal-minian." We think the choice is and can only be either A and B, but in God's creativity the third choice may be "dark chocolate." God truly thinks "outside the box."

C. S. Lewis writes about this freedom in the Garden of Eden where evil is unknown.

> Evil begins, in a universe where all was good, from free will, which was permitted because it makes possible the greatest good of all. The corruption of the first sinner consists not in choosing some evil thing (there are no evil things for him to choose) but in preferring a lesser good (himself) before a greater (God). The Fall is, in fact, Pride.[29]

Satan doesn't tempt Eve with evil, but with something that seemed very good. To become like her Creator:

> God knows that in the day you eat from [the forbidden tree] your eyes will be opened, and you will be like God, knowing good and evil. When the woman saw that the tree was good for food, and that it was a delight to the eyes, and that the tree was desirable to make *one* wise, she took from its fruit and ate; and she gave also to her husband with her, and he ate (Genesis 3:5-6).

Satan used the very same tactic with Jesus after he had gone without food for forty days and nights. The devil taunted, "If You are the Son of God, command that these stones become bread" (Matthew 4:3). We know that Jesus could multiply five loves of bread to feed five thousand men, not including women and children, so turning stones to bread—when he was starving—is not evil.

The enemy appealed to something good in both Eve and Jesus—but with a less-than-good motive: pride. To become *like* God. To prove he *was* God. And Jesus' final temptation offered a truly tempting offer:

> The people passing by shouted abuse, shaking their heads in mockery. "Look at you now!" they yelled at him. "You said you were going to destroy the Temple and rebuild it in three days. Well then, *if you are the Son of God, save yourself and come down from the cross!*"
>
> The leading priests, the teachers of religious law, and the elders also mocked Jesus. "He saved others," they scoffed, "but he can't save himself! So he is the King of Israel, is he? *Let him come down from the cross right now, and we will believe in him!*" (Matthew 27:39-42, author's emphasis).

For three years, Jesus had been praying that people would believe in him and the salvation he offered.

Satan has not changed his strategy from Genesis 3: Offer the right thing, the wrong way. Jesus came to be ruler of earth, so Satan offers that very thing. He "took Him to a very high mountain and showed Him all the kingdoms of the world and their glory; and he said to Him, 'All these things I will give You, if You fall down and worship me'" (Matthew 4:8-9).

And now, "Come down from the cross and we will believe in you."

God Wants What Is Best Through the Best Means

James, the brother of Jesus, makes it very clear that although we live in an unholy, evil world, God is holy and is never the source of evil:

> God blesses those who patiently endure testing and temptation. Afterward they will receive the crown of life that God

> has promised to those who love him. And remember, when you are being tempted, do not say, "God is tempting me." God is never tempted to do wrong, and he never tempts anyone else. Temptation comes from our own desires, which entice us and drag us away. These desires give birth to sinful actions. And when sin is allowed to grow, it gives birth to death.
>
> So don't be misled, my dear brothers and sisters. Whatever is good and perfect is a gift coming down to us from God our Father, who created all the lights in the heavens. He never changes or casts a shifting shadow (James 1:12-17).

Michelle Steele writes her miraculous story of coming from a life of sexual abuse, drug addiction, and being prostituted, to coming to Christ and becoming pastor of a growing church. In *The Guilt, the Shame, and the Blood,* she writes:

> Don't blame God for what that person did. God didn't do it. I am done with people blaming God for what happened to me. Well-meaning people have patted my hand and said, "God allowed all of those terrible things to happen to you so He could use you for His glory now." I want to scream in their face, "No!" God didn't plan for men to molest me. God didn't want me to be a prostitute. It didn't please God for me to spend years lost in a cloudy haze of drug addiction just so I could testify to drug addicts. I would never let

anything bad happen to my children so that they could be instrumental for me later. That would be child abuse!

God didn't allow or permit those things. God gave each person a free will. If a person commits a crime or violates the rights of another person, they chose to do it. God hated it when those men molested me. God hated it when grown men manipulated me and touched me in places that only my husband should touch me. It broke God's heart to see it happen. Unless those men repent and receive forgiveness for their guilt, God will punish them. But God didn't sit back and say, "Let it happen."[30]

People—Good and Bad—Are Affected by Evil

Contrary to what James and Pastor Steele write, there are people who believe that evil is a direct and divine punishment:

> About this time Jesus was informed that Pilate had murdered some people from Galilee as they were offering sacrifices at the Temple. "Do you think those Galileans were worse sinners than all the other people from Galilee?" Jesus asked. "Is that why they suffered? Not at all! And you will perish, too, unless you repent of your sins and turn to God. And what about the eighteen people who died when the tower in Siloam fell on them? Were they the worst sinners in Jerusalem? No, and I tell you again that unless you repent, you will perish, too" (Luke 13:1-5 NLT).

> As [Jesus] passed by, He saw a man blind from birth. And His disciples asked Him, "Rabbi, who sinned, this man or his parents, that he would be born blind?" Jesus answered, *"It was* neither *that* this man sinned, nor his parents; but *it was* so that the works of God might be displayed in him" (John 9:1-3).

It is true, however, that the Bible does teach there are very real consequences of our behavior.

Natural Consequences

> Do not be deceived, God is not mocked; for whatever a man sows, this he will also reap (Galatians 6:7).

> The wicked conceive evil; they are pregnant with trouble and give birth to lies. They dig a deep pit to trap others, then fall into it themselves. The trouble they make for others backfires on them. The violence they plan falls on their own heads (Psalm 7:15-16 NLT).

Both individuals, groups, and nations reap what they sow. Unfortunately, there are no "victimless crimes." The consequences of sin ripple well beyond the individual sinner. The prophet Nathan prophesies the consequences for David's adultery with Bathsheba and taking out a "hit" on her husband, Uriah:

> Nathan then said to David, "You are the man! Thus says the LORD God of Israel . . ."

> "Now therefore, the sword shall never depart from your house, because you

> have despised Me and have taken the wife of Uriah the Hittite to be your wife.' Thus says the LORD, 'Behold, I will raise up evil against you from your own household; I will even take your wives before your eyes and give *them* to your companion, and he will lie with your wives in broad daylight. Indeed you did it secretly, but I will do this thing before all Israel, and under the sun.'"
>
> "Because by this deed you have given occasion to the enemies of the LORD to blaspheme, the child also that is born to you shall surely die" (2 Samuel 12:7, 10-12, 14).

What follows makes "The Game of Thrones" look like "The Brady Bunch."

First David's son, Amnon, raped his step-sister, Tamar (2 Samuel 13). The son had learned from the father, "If you want something, go get it."

Absalom, David's son and Tamar's brother, killed Amnon, then fled town for three years. When Absalom returned to Jerusalem, David refused to see him.

Second, Absalom began campaigning for his father's throne by hanging out at the city gate offering to help citizens who were being ignored by his father (2 Samuel 15). Absalom recruited Ahithopel, formerly David's trusted advisor.

Third, once David realized his son was orchestrating a full-scale coup, the king fled Jerusalem, hoping to buy time to regroup. This set up another consequence that Nathan had precisely prophesied (2 Samuel 12:11-12):

> Ahithophel told [Absalom], "Go and sleep with your father's concubines, for he has left them here to look after the

> palace. Then all Israel will know that you have insulted your father beyond hope of reconciliation, and they will throw their support to you." So they set up a tent on the palace roof where everyone could see it, and Absalom went in and had sex with his father's concubines (2 Samuel 16:21-22 NLT).

David then sent his men against Absalom's army, but with explicit instructions not to harm his son. However, Absalom's luxurious locks got caught in the branches of an oak tree and his mule kept on going. Soon Joab came upon the king's rebellious offspring hanging by his hair.

> Then Joab said, "I will not waste time here with you." So he took three spears in his hand and thrust them through the heart of Absalom while he was yet alive in the midst of the oak. And ten young men who carried Joab's armor gathered around and struck Absalom and killed him (2 Samuel 18:14-15).

David returned to Jerusalem and attempted to regain control by enlisting his former enemies. He replaced Joab—the commander of his army, who had killed his son—with the commander of Absalom's army, Amasa. As David tried to put his kingdom back together, those from Israel felt left out with David favoring his family from Judah. This would later give birth to a serious split.

Was this dysfunctional and disastrous family a divine punishment or the result of natural consequences?

The Bible is very clear that we *do* reap what we sow. While God offers unconditional love and forgiveness, natural consequences will inevitably play out. Yes, David *was* "a man after God own heart," but his hormones got him into a world of trouble. Often there are physical consequences (sexually-transmitted diseases), legal consequences (fines, child support, incarceration) and relationship consequences (broken trust, restraining orders, the abused becoming abusers, etc.). We can be forgiven for our actions, but not necessarily for the reactions.

Children are *Not* Punished by God

Sexually transmitted disease in a mother can cause blindness in her baby. This is why the disciples asked, "'Who sinned, this man or his parents that he would be born blind?'" (John 9:2). And today, "crack babies" and children with fetal alcohol syndrome certainly suffer the consequences of their mother's actions during pregnancy. But the Bible is clear children are not divinely punished for the sins of their parents.

> Then another message came to me from the Lord: "Why do you quote this proverb concerning the land of Israel: 'The parents have eaten sour grapes, but their children's mouths pucker at the taste'? As surely as I live, says the Sovereign Lord, you will not quote this proverb anymore in Israel. For all people are mine to judge—both parents and children alike. And this is my rule: The person who sins is the one who will die.
>
> "What?" you ask. "Doesn't the child pay for the parent's sins?" No! For if the child does what is just and right and keeps my decrees, that child will surely live. The person who sins is the one who will die. The child will not be punished for the parent's sins, and the parent will not be punished for the child's sins. Righteous people will be rewarded for their own righteous behavior, and wicked people will be punished for their own wickedness. But if wicked

> people turn away from all their sins and begin to obey my decrees and do what is just and right, they will surely live and not die. All their past sins will be forgotten, and they will live because of the righteous things they have done.
>
> "Do you think that I like to see wicked people die? says the Sovereign Lord" (Ezekiel 18:1-4, 19-23 NLT).

Because God is holy, the apostle Paul is very clear that we can't take disobedience lightly.

> What shall we say then? Are we to continue in sin so that grace may increase? May it never be! How shall we who died to sin still live in it? (Romans 6:1-2)
>
> You are now ashamed of the things you used to do, things that end in eternal doom. But now you are free from the power of sin and have become slaves of God. Now you do those things that lead to holiness and result in eternal life. For the wages of sin is death, but the free gift of God is eternal life through Christ Jesus our Lord (Romans 6:21b-23).

Paul is not talking about what my boyhood church called "deep sin." There is no "Sin Lite!" But there are several Greek words which can be translated "sin."

Adikia, is often translated "sin," but it more accurately describes an action that is "a perversion of righteousness." The person who *adikia*-s has lost sensitivity to God and views immoral actions as completely normal, even righteous. Calling good evil and evil good (Isaiah 5:20).

Anomia is not the occasional woops-I'm-sorry-God-I-won't-let-it-happen-again sin, but describes a lifestyle of sin. Just as fish understands no other life than swimming, *anomia*-ers understand no other life than sinning.

Asebia deals specifically with rebellion toward or rejection of God. The apostle Paul uses the word when he describes ungodliness in Romans 1:18-32, 2 Timothy 2:16, and Titus 2:12.

Hamartia is the Greek word in the verses from Romans 6 above. It describes actions and attitudes that "fall short" of God's perfection. We *hamartia* whenever our actions and attitudes are not completely God-like.

Luke uses *hamartia* in his version of the Lord's Prayer: "Forgive us our *hamartia*-s for we also forgive everyone who *hamartia*-s against us" (Luke 11:4). Christ, therefore, implies that his followers do sin—fairly regularly.

John is even more direct:

> If we claim we have no sin [*hamaria*], we are only fooling ourselves and not living in the truth. But if we confess our sins to him, he is faithful and just to forgive us our sins and to cleanse us from all wickedness. If we claim we have not sinned, we are calling God a liar and showing that his word has no place in our hearts (1 John 1:8-10 NLT).

God is holy. And unholy things happen when people reject him. And those unholy actions reap consequences on the sinner, and unfortunately those consequences affect completely innocent people.

Asaph and the entire nation certainly struggled with the consequences from the sins of David, Solomon, and his sons. But Asaph can rejoice that despite humanity's sins, God is in control and worthy to be praised:

The Mighty One, God, the Lord, *has spoken,*
And summoned the earth from the rising of the sun to its setting.
Out of Zion, the perfection of beauty,
God has shone forth.
May our God come and not keep silence;
Fire devours before Him,
And it is very tempestuous around Him.
He summons the heavens above,
And the earth, to judge His people:
"Gather My godly ones to Me,
Those who have made a covenant with Me by sacrifice."
And the heavens declare His righteousness,
For God Himself is judge.
Psalm 50:1-6

9

Why Doesn't God Seem to Prevent Evil?

O God, the nations have invaded Your inheritance;
They have defiled Your holy temple;
They have laid Jerusalem in ruins.
They have given the dead bodies of Your servants
for food to the birds of the heavens,
The flesh of Your godly ones to the beasts of the earth.
They have poured out their blood like water round about Jerusalem;
And there was no one to bury them.
We have become a reproach to our neighbors,
A scoffing and derision to those around us.
How long, O LORD?
Psalm 79:1-5a

Hopefully, I've made the case, in the previous chapter, that God is not the *creator* or *cause* of evil, but it doesn't answer the question why God doesn't *prevent* evil.

The September 11, 2001, terrorist attacks killed more than three thousand innocent men, women, and children, raising questions of why didn't God prevent the attack.

There were numerous warning signs that could have prevented the tragedy. As early as January 1995, a terrorist was arrested in the Philippines and confessed to plans to crash a plane into a U. S. federal building. In May 1998, a Federal Bureau of Investigations agent wrote a memo noting he was concerned about a number of Middle Eastern men seeking flight training in Oklahoma City. (They seemed more interested in flying than taking off and landing.) However, the memo was never sent to FBI headquarters. In December 1998, the Federal Aviation Administration warned airlines and airports that Osama bin Laden had made plans to hijack commercial aircraft on the East coast. In July 2001, an FBI agent wrote a memo about foreigners training at area flight schools, and the Federal Aviation Administration warned airlines about terrorists possibly hijacking commercial aircraft. And, on September 10, 2001, the National Security Agency intercepted two communications from Afghanistan to Saudi Arabia: "Tomorrow is zero hour" and "The match begins tomorrow." The messages were not translated until September 12.

Couldn't God have assisted these agencies in stopping the attack? After all, he works through nations and governments (Romans 13:1-4).

Furthermore, I've flown on thousands of flights and probably experienced hundreds of canceled or delayed flights due to weather, mechanical issues, or simply pilots not getting their required hours of sleep. The morning of September 11 dawned with clear skies—perfect weather for flying. Couldn't God have stopped these flights through any number of methods?

Asaph certainly struggled with this question:

> O God, do not remain quiet; Do not be
> silent and, O God, do not be still. For

behold, Your enemies make an uproar, And those who hate You have exalted themselves. They make shrewd plans against Your people, And conspire together against Your treasured ones. They have said, "Come, and let us wipe them out as a nation, That the name of Israel be remembered no more." For they have conspired together with one mind; Against You they make a covenant (Psalm 83:1-5).

These questions reverberated throughout Central Indiana when Amanda Blackburn, a popular pastor's wife, was sexually assaulted and fatally shot in a home invasion while her husband, Davey, was at the gym. She was pregnant with the couple's second child. It struck me particularly hard since Davey's parents and his aunt were in my youth group during the 80s.

The national media picked up the story:

Amanda didn't have an enemy in the world. I can't imagine any reason why. That's why this has baffled us as much as anybody. It's really hard to sort through all of the emotions of what we're feeling about all this. We're confused. We don't understand why. We're angry. We're not really sure what to do.

I read Amanda's journal entry just a few days before—she journaled every day of her life. Just a few days before she was killed, she put something in there that just spoke volumes to us that we're deriving strength from. She said, "We don't know what the future holds but we know who holds the future

> and that's Jesus." We're drawing our strength from that and we know that Jesus holds the future and we can't see it clearly but she sees it clearly now because she's in heaven with Jesus and we'll see her soon.[31]
>
> Though everything inside of me wants to hate, be angry, and slip into despair I choose the route of forgiveness, grace and hope. . . .[32]

Davey also stated that he has already forgiven the men who allegedly murdered his wife.

> I don't want to live my life going down the path of bitterness because it will destroy my soul and it will destroy everybody around me if I choose [unforgiveness].
>
> So today, I choose forgiveness. And tomorrow, I pray that I can wake up and choose forgiveness by the power of Jesus Christ. One of the things about Jesus, when they were inflicting way more pain than any of us can imagine on him, on the cross, he looked out and he said, "Father, forgive them, for they don't know what they're doing." And so that spirit lives in us and we're just praying His spirit would help us in that.[33]
>
> What was so great about Amanda is that she was so selfless that she didn't want her life to be put on display, ever, but

> she wanted Jesus to be put on display. We feel like that's what happened at the celebration service, that Jesus was lifted up and people's lives have been changed because of that.[34]

The Blackburn family has chosen not to dwell on the "what ifs." What if the serial burglar had been captured a day earlier? What if Davey had chosen not to go to the gym that morning? What if . . . ?"

They have chosen to view this horrendous abuse of freewill as an opportunity to share the wonderful freedom from hate and vengeance that can only be found in freely loving God and others.

My friend, John Bray, dean of chapel at Indiana Wesleyan University, has this answer when someone asks, "Why doesn't God prevent evil?" Actually, his answer is another question:

> "Where would he stop?" That's the question I've learned to ask people who are wrestling with God's fairness.
>
> If there is evil then there must also be good. But the root of evil is sin. And "all have sinned" (Romans 3:23). That means there is a touch of evil in me—and you.
>
> We think God should do something. Don't allow Hitler. Don't allow ISIS. Don't allow the drunk to get behind the wheel. Wipe them out.
>
> But where would he stop? To wipe out evil, God would have to wipe out sin; and to wipe out sin means he would wipe out me—and you.[35]

John is absolutely right. All of us fall within the spectrum of "evil." To illustrate this, one morning at the church Lois and I were pastoring, I asked a young man to stand to the left of the platform to represent Adolph Hitler. On the far right, I asked a young woman to play the part of Mother Teresa. Then I asked each person in the audience to mentally place themselves on the platform somewhere between the symbols of evil and sainthood.

"None of us are perfect, but I'm fairly certain that you placed yourself closer to Mother Teresa than Adolph Hitler. We're not saints, but we're not the personification of evil either. So, where do you think you rank in comparison to God? We're in this church in central Indiana, but do you know where God is on the spectrum? He's enjoying a parade of penguins in Antarctica.

"So in comparison, we all are far closer to Adolph Hitler than to God. And even Mother Teresa is just thirty feet from *der Feuer* compared to God who is ten-thousand miles away. In our unsaved state, we are infinitely evil compared to an infinitely holy God."

Paul writes about feeling superior to Adolph Hitler, radical terrorists, or serial killers:

> You may think you can condemn such people, but you are just as bad, and you have no excuse! When you say they are wicked and should be punished, you are condemning yourself, for you who judge others do these very same things. And we know that God, in his justice, will punish anyone who does such things. Since you judge others for doing these things, why do you think you can avoid God's judgment when you do the same things? Don't you see how wonderfully kind, tolerant, and patient God is with you? Does this mean nothing to you? Can't you see that his kindness is intended to turn you from your sin? (Romans 2:1-4 NLT).

I am glad that I am under the forgiveness and mercy of a holy God. And Asaph was comforted that, although he couldn't understand the evil he was witnessing, he believed that God had also seen it and was not ignoring it.

But to the wicked God says,
"What right have you to tell of My statutes
And to take My covenant in your mouth?
"For you hate discipline,
And you cast My words behind you.
"When you see a thief, you are pleased with him,
And you associate with adulterers.
"You let your mouth loose in evil
And your tongue frames deceit.
"You sit and speak against your brother;
You slander your own mother's son.
"These things you have done and I kept silence;
You thought that I was just like you;
I will reprove you and state the case *in order before your eyes."*
Psalm 50:16-21

10

Why Is God Slow in Bringing Judgment?

*Why should pagan nations be allowed to scoff,
asking, "Where is their God?"
Show us your vengeance against the nations,
for they have spilled the blood of your servants.
Listen to the moaning of the prisoners.
Demonstrate your great power by saving those condemned to die.
O Lord, pay back our neighbors seven times
for the scorn they have hurled at you.
Then we your people, the sheep of your pasture,
will thank you forever and ever,
praising your greatness from generation to generation.*
Psalm 79:10-13

How long will you judge unjustly
And show partiality to the wicked?
Vindicate the weak and fatherless;
Do justice to the afflicted and destitute.
Rescue the weak and needy;
Deliver them out of the hand of the wicked.
Psalm 82:2-4

Every newscast provides ample opportunities to ask why God is slow in bringing judgment to ISIS suicide bombers, child sexual predators, corporate criminals who have bankrupted pension funds, and . . . the list of crimes goes on and on.

In the Old Testament, and on two occasions in the New, God's judgments were swift. But Paul explains why God is no longer in the "smiting" business:

> For God presented Jesus as the sacrifice for sin. People are made right with God when they believe that Jesus sacrificed his life, shedding his blood. This sacrifice shows that God was being fair when he held back and did not punish those who sinned in times past, for he was looking ahead and including them in what he would do in this present time. God did this to demonstrate his righteousness, for he himself is fair and just, and he makes sinners right in his sight when they believe in Jesus (Romans 3:25-26 NLT).

God's righteous and just requirement of death for sin is lovingly—and brutally—fulfilled in the death of the Son of God.

The psalmist notes "the godly will rejoice when they see injustice avenged. Then at last everyone will say, 'There is a God who judges justly here on earth'" (Psalm 58:10-11). I think the psalmist would be surprised how that would be fulfilled:

> God showed how much he loved us by sending his one and only Son into the world so that we might have eternal life through him. This is real love—not that we loved God, but that he loved us and sent his Son as a sacrifice to take away our sins (1 John 4:9-10).

When Osama bin Laden was finally tracked down and killed in Pakistan ten years after 9/11, many Christians took to social media to praise God for his death. I was conflicted. Yes, justice was finally served, but I was also reminded of Ezekiel 18:23: "Do you think that I like to see wicked people die? says the Sovereign Lord. Of course not! I want them to turn from their wicked ways and live" (NLT).

David understood the frustration of watching evil apparently triumph over righteousness. He was anointed king as a teenager, but spent his early adulthood running for his life from King Saul. While the wicked king was in the palace, David was hiding out in caves. And while David was trying to sooth the madman with his harp playing, the king was using God's anointed for javelin practice. And, although, David had opportunities to kill Saul, he refused and left justice in God's hands.

Later, in Psalm 37, David provides counsel in responding to apparently unpunished evil:

Don't fret

> Do not fret because of evildoers (37:1).

> Rest in the Lord and wait patiently for Him; Do not fret because of him who prospers in his way, Because of the man who carries out wicked schemes. Cease from anger and forsake wrath; Do not fret; *it leads* only to evildoing (37:7-8b).

I grew up in a family of world-class fretters. My parents fretted about World War II and the Korean conflict. And I grew up fretting about the Cold War where, in addition to school fire and tornado drills, we practiced survival from a nuclear attack from the Soviet Union. We would all dive under our desks—as if a half-inch of plywood and laminate could stop a thermo-nuclear warhead. "Entertainment" at church carry-in dinners often included Civil Defense films detailing how to build your own bomb shelter. My children and grandchildren have grown up under the fear of terrorism. Jesus expands on David's command, "Do not fret; *it leads* only to evildoing."

> "I say to you, do not be worried about your life, *as to* what you will eat or what you will drink; nor for your body, *as to* what you will put on. Is not life more than food, and the body more than clothing? Look at the birds of the air, that they do not sow, nor reap nor gather into barns, and *yet* your heavenly Father feeds them. Are you not worth much more than they? And who of you by being worried can add a *single* hour to his life? And why are you worried about clothing? Observe how the lilies of the field grow; they do not toil nor do they spin, yet I say to you that not even Solomon in all his glory clothed himself like one of these. But if God so clothes the grass of the field, which is *alive* today and tomorrow is thrown into the furnace, *will He* not much more *clothe* you? You of little faith! Do not worry then, saying, 'What will we eat?' or 'What will we drink?' or 'What will we wear for clothing?' For the Gentiles eagerly seek all these things; for your heavenly Father

> knows that you need all these things,
> But seek first His kingdom and His righteousness, and all these things will be added to you" (Matthew 6:25-31).

Worry assumes that our Heavenly Father won't provide for our basic necessities. "You of little faith!" (Matthew 8:26).

Worry doesn't "add a single hour to [our] life" (Matthew 6:27). Corrie ten Boom puts it well: "Worry does not empty tomorrow of its sorrow, it empties today of its strength."

Worry is disobedience to Jesus' direct command "Do not worry."

Finally, worry is a sign of wrong priorities. Your Heavenly Father knows you need food, drink and clothing, so "seek first His kingdom and His righteousness, and all these things will be added to you" (Matthew 6:33).

I'm slowly learning that it takes as much emotional energy to fret as it does to trust, so I'm going to choose to trust.

Don't envy

> . . . neither be envious against those who work unrighteousness (Psalm 37:1).

> Be not envious toward wrongdoers (Psalm 37:8a).

Jeanette shares her story of envying her ex-husband's successes.

> I could barely breathe when I heard my ex-husband's girlfriend was now his fiancée. It didn't shock me. I'd expected him to be one of those guys who got remarried as soon as he was legally free to. But his news still sent me reeling.

He'd abandoned me and our two sons.

My youngest son and I were now living with my parents, and my oldest, a young adult, was two hundred miles away in the city we'd had to leave behind.

Through the entire divorce process, I'd been waiting for God to rain his justice on my very unjust situations. I consoled myself that the perfect Judge was in control, and that none of us really got away with anything. In other words, I'd been waiting for my ex-husband to get his.

After all I'd been through, *I* deserved to find someone while *he* spent the rest of his days alone, jobless, homeless, and disliked by everybody.

And yet, I had spent two years watching my heavenly Father provide, seeing his people at their best, and finding strength to endure what would have slayed me in the past. He'd empowered me to be gracious and forgiving when it made more sense to lash out. Yes, I'd had to completely start over, but the life I was building for myself and my son was stable and good.

I believed that God was still the perfect judge—that his justice and my idea of justice might look very different—even when my ex-husband seemed to be thriving or getting away with what he shouldn't. Each time God reminds me to focus on what he was doing in me rather than what he was or wasn't doing to someone else. And each time. I feel less bent on seeing evidence that the person who hurt me got punished, and more like the person that he equipped to get through a very painful time with grace.[36]

Don't get angry

David warns, "Cease from anger and forsake wrath (37:8). However, in his early days, his psalms were full and overflowing with anger toward his enemies. Here's just one of the many examples:

> Let his children be fatherless And his wife a widow.
> Let his children wander about and beg; And let them seek sustenance far from their ruined homes.
> Let the creditor seize all that he has, And let strangers plunder the product of his labor.
> Let there be none to extend lovingkindness to him,
> Nor any to be gracious to his fatherless children (Psalm 109:9-12).

Jesus, however, reinforces the more mature David's command to not be angry.

> "You have heard the law that says, 'Love your neighbor' and hate your enemy. But I say, love your enemies! Pray for those who persecute you! In that

way, you will be acting as true children of your Father in heaven. For he gives his sunlight to both the evil and the good, and he sends rain on the just and the unjust alike" (Matthew 5:43-45 NLT).

Depart from evil, do good

> Depart from evil and do good,
> So you will abide forever (Psalm 37:27).

I love the ways that churches and Christian organization put into practice the apostle Paul's admonition to "overcome evil with good" (Romans 12:21).

Instead of rioting against the cruel conditions in England during the 1700s, John Wesley and his "Methodists" set up free clinics, opened the first employees' credit union, and revolutionized the country. And did it without the bloodshed of the American and French revolutions.

Instead of calling pro-abortionists "baby killers," pro-life supporters began setting up Crisis Pregnancy Centers which provided compassionate care for pregnant women by offering her testing, maternity clothes, and baby supplies. Crisis Pregnancy Centers now outnumber abortion providers, and the abortion rate is declining.

Instead of complaining about Hollywood movies, a group of believers has established Act One: Writing for Hollywood conferences to raise up Christians in the industry.

Prison Fellowship, rather than complaining about crime, has become active in justice issues. But most important, thousands of volunteers are taking the Christian message into prisons and discipling converted convicts.

The whole point of overcoming evil with good is to provide a positive, godly alternative to the evil.

Rest in the Lord

> Rest in the LORD and wait patiently for him (37:7).

I'm one of those people who impatiently taps his foot during the sixty seconds the microwave heats a cup of soup. I drum the steering wheel with my thumbs, waiting for a red light to turn green. And even though I remember "dial up" Internet connections, my cable connection is always a nano-second too slow for me.

But worse, I try to hurry God along. (That is as futile—and foolish—as a husband waiting for his wife in the car to honk the horn.)

> There is an appointed time for everything. And there is a time for every event under heaven (Ecclesiastes 3:1).

> For since the world began, no ear has heard and no eye has seen a God like you, who works for those who wait for him! (Isaiah 64:4 NLT).

> Let us not lose heart in doing good, for in due time we will reap if we do not grow weary (Galatians 6:9).

God's timing never seems to coincide with my schedule—but it is always perfect.

Wait for God to Bring Judgment

There is an entire category of psalms labeled "imprecatory," in which the writers call down judgment upon their enemies. And Asaph certainly poured out his contempt for his enemies.

> [May God's enemies become] as dung for the ground.
>
> O my God, make them like the whirling dust,
>
> Like chaff before the wind.

> Like fire that burns the forest
> And like a flame that sets the mountains on fire,
> So pursue them with Your tempest
> And terrify them with Your storm.
> Fill their faces with dishonor,
> That they may seek Your name, O Lord.
> Let them be ashamed and dismayed forever,
> And let them be humiliated and perish
> (Psalm 83:10b, 13-17).

Keep in mind that poetry tends to be hyperbolic. Poets will climb the highest mountain, swim the deepest sea, traverse the hottest desert for their beloved.

David, older and wiser than in his younger warrior days, writes in Psalm 37:8 to "Cease from anger and forsake wrath; Do not fret; *it leads* only to evildoing."

Paul also makes this clear:

> Never pay back evil with more evil. Do things in such a way that everyone can see you are honorable. Do all that you can to live in peace with everyone.
>
> Dear friends, never take revenge. Leave that to the righteous anger of God (Romans 12:17-19 NLT).

God *Will* Bring Judgment

God's judgment is slow, but it is sure. Psalm 37 declares:

> Transgressors will be altogether destroyed; The posterity of the wicked will be cut off. But the salvation of the righteous is from the Lord; He

is their strength in time of trouble. The LORD helps them and delivers them; He delivers them from the wicked and saves them, Because they take refuge in Him (37:38-40, see also vs 9-17).

Throughout the Old Testament, we see swift justice. In the third chapter of the Bible. Adam and Eve are cursed with mortality and banished from the Garden of Eden. In the sixth chapter, God wiped out all life except for Noah's family and a boat load of animals.

In the next book, God poured out ten plagues on the Egyptian people when Pharaoh refused to set the Israelites free from slavery. And he brought swift punishment on his own people when they worshiped the golden calf (Exodus 32). The earth opened and swallowed those who rebelled against Moses (Numbers 16). Bears killed young men who insulted the prophet Elisa's bald head *(2 Kings 2:23–24)*.

And swift justice continued through the early chapters of Acts:

> But there was a certain man named Ananias who, with his wife, Sapphira, sold some property. He brought part of the money to the apostles, claiming it was the full amount. With his wife's consent, he kept the rest.
>
> Then Peter said, "Ananias, why have you let Satan fill your heart? You lied to the Holy Spirit, and you kept some of the money for yourself. The property was yours to sell or not sell, as you wished. And after selling it, the money was also yours to give away. How could you do a thing like this? You weren't lying to us but to God!"
>
> As soon as Ananias heard these words, he fell to the floor and died. Everyone who heard about it was terrified. Then

> some young men got up, wrapped him in a sheet, and took him out and buried him (Acts 5:1-6).

About three hours later, the same judgment fell on Sapphira. No wonder, Luke writes: "Great fear gripped the entire church and everyone else who heard what had happened" (Acts 5:11).

Then, five chapters later, when a delegation from Tyre and Sidon arrived . . .

> Herod [Agrippa] put on his royal robes, sat on his throne, and made a speech to them. The people gave him a great ovation, shouting, "It's the voice of a god, not of a man!"
>
> Instantly, an angel of the Lord struck Herod with a sickness, because he accepted the people's worship instead of giving the glory to God. So he was consumed with worms and died (Acts 12:21-23 NLT).

This is the last recorded incident of God bringing swift and certain death sentence in the biblical past. However, it is clear that at some point in the future, God will once again actively judge sin:

> "The Son of Man will send forth His angels, and they will gather out of His kingdom all stumbling blocks, and those who commit lawlessness, and will throw them into the furnace of fire; in that place there will be weeping and gnashing of teeth" (Matthew 13:41-42).

> And God will provide rest for you who are being persecuted and also for us when the Lord Jesus appears from heaven. He will come with his mighty angels (2 Thessalonians 1:6-7 NLT).

But best of all . . .

God Will Bring Redemption

One of most amazing examples of God "not wanting anyone to perish, but to come to eternal life" is Jeffrey Lionel Dahmer. This American serial killer and sex offender raped, tortured, murdered, dismembered, and ate parts of seventeen men and boys between 1978 and 1991.

Although he was diagnosed with borderline personality disorder as well as schizo-typical personality and psychotic disorder, he was found legally sane for trial and convicted of sixteen murders and sentenced to fifteen terms of life imprisonment.

A Wisconsin pastor, Roy Ratcliff, began weekly visits with this notorious felon. In Ratcliff's book, *Dark Journey, Deep Grace,* he describes Dahmer's conversion to Christ. Surprisingly, the pastor received such responses as "If Jeffrey Dahmer is going to heaven, then I don't want to be there." Ratcliff writes:

> How can a Christian hold that viewpoint? I don't understand it. Does it come from a misunderstanding of the forgiveness of sin? Is forgiveness limited to those who are not very bad after all? Is there no joy in knowing that a sinner has turned to God?
>
> Jeff was a sinner. His life proves there is no limit to our capacity to sin or be cruel to other people. We are all candidates for murder and mayhem.

> It doesn't take crazy people to do such things. . . . I believe any of us are capable of everything Jeff did, if we leave God out of our lives.[37]

But God's love for his creation is infinite and includes what society—and unfortunately some in the church—judge as unredeemable.

So, why does God seem slow in dispensing judgment? Because he always balances justice with his mercy—and Jesus tips the scales! Despite the evil Asaph was witnessing, he could write:

> *For, behold, those who are far from You will perish;*
> *You have destroyed all those who are unfaithful to You.*
> *But as for me, the nearness of God is my good;*
> *I have made the Lord GOD my refuge,*
> *That I may tell of all Your works.*
> Psalm 73:27-28

> *Fill their faces with dishonor,*
> *That they may seek Your name, O LORD.*
> *Let them be ashamed and dismayed forever,*
> *And let them be humiliated and perish,*
> *That they may know that You alone, whose name is the LORD,*
> *Are the Most High over all the earth.*
> Psalm 83:16-18

Answers

11

Life is Hard

The enemy has damaged everything within the sanctuary.
Your adversaries have roared in the midst of Your meeting place;
They have set up their own standards for signs.
It seems as if one had lifted up
His axe in a forest of trees.
And now all its carved work
They smash with hatchet and hammers.
They have burned Your sanctuary to the ground;
They have defiled the dwelling place of Your name.
They said in their heart, "Let us completely subdue them."
They have burned all the meeting places of God in the land.
Psalm 74:4-8

I love how M. Scott Peck begins his best-selling book, *The Road Less Traveled:*

> Life is difficult. This is a great truth, one of the greatest truths. It is a great truth because once we truly see this truth, we transcend it. Once we truly know that life is difficult—once we truly understand and accept it—then life is no longer difficult. Because once it is accepted, the fact that life is difficult no longer matters.[38]

Let me rephrase that. I hate the way Peck begins his book, because I dislike the concept that life's default setting is "difficult."

The apostle Peter wrote the same sentiment nearly two thousand years ago, "Beloved, *do not be surprised* at the fiery ordeal among you, which comes upon you for your testing, as though some strange thing were happening to you" (1 Peter 4:12, *author's emphasis*). Life without difficulty is what is surprising!

John Piper writes that he has "a growing sense that suffering is normal and useful and [an] essential element in Christian life and ministry.[39]" Or as Barbara Johnson poignantly puts it in her book, *Splashes of Joy in the Cesspools of Life*, "We are Easter people living in a Good Friday World!"[40] This should not be surprising. Jesus, who promised his followers an "abundant" life, lived a hard life. Let's look at the evidence:

Despised, rejected, a man of sorrows

Life was certainly "difficult" for Jesus.

> He was despised and rejected—a man of sorrows, acquainted with deepest grief. We turned our backs on him and looked the other way. He was despised, and we did not care (Isaiah 53:3 NLT).

> Once again the people picked up stones to kill him. Jesus said, "At my Father's direction I have done many good works. For which one are you going to stone me?"
>
> They replied, "We're stoning you not for any good work, but for blasphemy! You, a mere man, claim to be God" (John 10:31-33).

Accused of being satanic

The holy Son of God was slandered to the point of being called demonic when he healed a blind man who couldn't speak:

> But when the Pharisees heard about the miracle, they said, "No wonder he can cast out demons. He gets his power from Satan, the prince of demons" (Matthew 12:24).

Thought to be crazy

Not even Jesus own family respected him: "His family thought he was crazy. 'He's out of his mind,' they said" (Mark 3:21 NLT). That's encouraging as many world-changers were initially thought to be out of their mind.

Homeless

Add to all this, Jesus lamented, "'Foxes have dens to live in, and birds have nests, but the Son of Man has no place even to lay his head'" (Matthew 8:20 NLT).

Brutally tortured and killed

The Gospel of Mark coldly describes his excruciating torture and execution:

> The soldiers took Jesus into the courtyard of the governor's headquarters . . . wove thorn branches into a crown and put it on his head. And they struck him on the head with a reed stick and spit on him. . . . Then they led him away to be crucified.
>
> [Jesus carried his cross] to a place called Golgotha (which means "Place of the Skull"). They offered him wine drugged with myrrh, but he refused it.
>
> Then the soldiers nailed him to the cross (15:16-17, 20, 22-24 NLT).

The apostle Paul also experienced his share of suffering:

> Five different times the Jewish leaders gave me thirty-nine lashes. Three times I was beaten with rods. Once I was stoned. Three times I was shipwrecked. Once I spent a whole night and a day adrift at sea. I have traveled on many long journeys. I have faced danger from rivers and from robbers. I have faced danger from my own people, the Jews, as well as from the Gentiles. I have faced danger in the cities, in the deserts, and on the seas. And I have faced danger from men who claim to be believers but are not. I have worked hard and long, enduring many sleepless nights. I have been hungry and thirsty and have often gone without food. I have shivered in the cold, without enough clothing to keep me warm (2 Corinthians 11:24-27 NLT).

And yet, as children in Sunday school, we sang songs about 'apple red happiness, popcorn cheerfulness,' and a 'gumdrop holiday' in the Lord. As a result, my little second-grade soul was shaken when my Sunday school teacher hanged herself one Saturday night.

She taught us how Peter miraculously was freed from prison—awaiting execution, but not the verses before when James was beheaded. We learned about Daniel being spared from the hungry lions, but never about early Christians being eaten alive by the animals in the Coliseum. All of our stories had "apple red happiness" endings! (Okay, having a headless James in a Bible picture book might be "too intense for young audiences.")

I wonder if she bought into the lie that life was supposed to be filled with "happiness," and when it wasn't, she despaired of life itself.

Here's my point. The Bible is not filled with "popcorn cheerfulness"—and neither is modern-day life. We live in a fallen world filled with disease, crime, carnivorous animals, natural disasters, etc. Life *is* difficult and the sooner we admit that, the sooner we can learn how to successfully cope in this world.

A friend from college was not having a "gumdrop holiday" when she sent this email to a small group of friends to describe her Stage 4 cancer:

> I got a call from the radiation department, and they've canceled my treatments this week because my blood work numbers have crashed again and are below 2. I am on the verge of tears. I keep reminding myself that God is in control, and I'm really okay with that, but I am so very disappointed!
>
> I have spent most of today trying to talk myself out of this feeling of despair. I've tried praying and I've even listened to a sermon or two from those who found out what happened and know how very upset I am. This entire experience

> [for the last year] has been a lot like a roller coaster ride that never ends—and tonight I just want to get off. I know that I'm going to continue this fight and I'm not giving up, but I'm just so tired and I'm on emotional overload.
>
> My mind has gone several times today to the story in the Bible (Exodus 17:8-12) where Aaron and Hur held up Moses' hands throughout the day so that the Israelites would win in their battle with Amalek and his army. Today, I am tired and weak spiritually and emotionally, and I need you to hold up my hands.
>
> I thank you in advance for being at my side![41]

That same week, her sister sent me a personal email:

> Just had a special time, just lying in bed talking to God, being transparent, telling him how I feel alone, abandoned, that I love him, but don't feel his love. That I know he cares for me. Then why have you either put me in this painful/ugly place of mental illness? Did I get any answers? NO! Do I feel better? Only to the point that I said what needed to be said. Tell you what, Jim, I am feeling like the writers of many of the psalms. Why have you left me? What do you want me to do? What do you want me to say? Will I get the answers? Gotta vent![42]

Here are excerpts from my response to my college friend's sister:

> You're in good company with Job, David, Asaph, Elijah, and all the other depressed Bible characters. Also, keep in mind, Jesus gave us a promise that never, ever fails:
>
> "I have told you these things, so that in me you may have peace. In this world you will have trouble. But take heart! I have overcome the world" (John 16:33). Jesus saves, but we live in a world that is lost.

I taught about that "promise" from John 16 one Sunday morning in January.

Immediately after the closing prayer, one family went out into the sub-zero weather to find that they had left the van's lights on and their battery was dead. Another family discovered their four-year-old had gotten into their van, turned it on, and backed it over a parking bumper. The worship leader went home to find her husband gone with a note telling her he wanted a divorce.

That night the church's hot-water-heating pipes froze up and the parsonage's furnace caught fire. Monday morning, a parishioner offered to thaw out the church's pipes with a blow torch—and caught the building's sub-flooring on fire. Then things got worse!

Yep, in this world we *will* have trouble. But there is hope at the end of the verse: "Take heart, Jesus has overcome the world." That's why Paul can write:

> We have this treasure in jars of clay to show that this all-surpassing power is from God and not from us. We are hard pressed on every side, but not crushed; perplexed, but not in despair; persecuted, but not abandoned; struck down, but not destroyed. We always carry around in

our body the death of Jesus, so that the life of Jesus may also be revealed in our body. For we who are alive are always being given over to death for Jesus' sake, so that his life may also be revealed in our mortal body. (2 Corinthians 4:7-11).

Here's the bottom line. I've centered it and put it in boldface with an exclamation point so its truth will stand out.

> **Life is not designed to make us happy.**
> **Life is designed to make us holy!**

Peter Kreeft writes: "The point of our lives in this world is not comfort, security, or even happiness, but training; not fulfillment but preparation. It's a lousy home, but it's a fine gymnasium.[43]"

Even Jesus learned to live a holy life through a hard life: "So even though Jesus was God's Son, he learned obedience from the things he suffered" (Hebrews 5:8 NLT).

Amazing! The very Son of God learned to be more like, well, God by the things he suffered. Was Jesus, as Isaiah writes, "despised and rejected by men, a man of sorrows, and familiar with suffering" (53:3) because he obeyed his Father? Or did he obey his Father because he learned by being "despised and rejected by men, a man of sorrows, and familiar with suffering?"

A psalmist wrote about this inconvenient truth:

> I used to wander off until you disciplined me; but now I closely follow your word. You are good and do only good; teach me your decrees.
>
> My suffering was good for me, for it taught me to pay attention to your decrees (Psalm 119:67-68, 71).

That is so true. I wrote in *Squeezing Good Out of Bad*:

> When I think back to my "successful" years—award-winning author and editor, world-traveling conference speaker, denominational executive, and co-pastor of a growing church—I certainly didn't resemble the Christ I was trying to follow. It has only been during my "failure" years—years between book contracts, estranged relationships, being voted out of a church, and having to borrow money to make a living writing and speaking—that I have come to derive my self-identity and self-worth from simply being a loved child of God.

Being a person of hope doesn't mean you're happy, carefree, or delusional. It means you look at life realistically, but with the knowledge that faith, hope, and love will eventually prevail over doubt, despair, and hate.

My friend, Bill Sweeney, has every human reason to be in despair with the hard life he finds himself living. And yet, on his blog, "Unshakeable Hope," he shares encouragement.

> At the age of thirty-five, I was diagnosed with ALS ("Lou Gehrig's Disease"). I'm now completely paralyzed and unable to speak. I'm writing this using a special computer that allows me to type using eye movements like Stephen Hawking.
>
> After being diagnosed, I was forced to go on disability; we had to sell our home and even our car. With medical bills and credit cards, within a year we

accumulated over $55,000 in debt. Three lawyers advised us to file for bankruptcy, but, after my wife and I prayed about it, we decided we'd trust God to help us instead. He did help us and continues to be faithful; He's proven that Philippians 4:19 is true!

The only thing I'm physically able to do is type, and I want to encourage believers that God really can bring them through any trial; I know what it's like to get a terminal diagnosis, to lose a good job, to be drowning in debt, and to battle depression, etc. I simply want to encourage people.[44]

Life is hard, but God is good! Asaph believed that.

> *"I warned the proud, 'Stop your boasting!'*
> *I told the wicked, 'Don't raise your fists!*
> *Don't raise your fists in defiance at the heavens*
> *or speak with such arrogance.'"*
> *For no one on earth—from east or west,*
> *or even from the wilderness—*
> *should raise a defiant fist.*
> *It is God alone who judges;*
> *he decides who will rise and who will fall.*
> *For the LORD holds a cup in his hand*
> *that is full of foaming wine mixed with spices.*
> *He pours out the wine in judgment,*
> *and all the wicked must drink it,*
> *draining it to the dregs.*
> *But as for me, I will always proclaim what God has done;*
> *I will sing praises to the God of Jacob.*
> *For God says, "I will break the strength of the wicked,*
> *but I will increase the power of the godly."*
> Psalm 75:4-10 NLT

12

God Is Good

*But [God], being compassionate, forgave
their iniquity and did not destroy them;
And often He restrained His anger
And did not arouse all His wrath.
Thus He remembered that they were but flesh,
A wind that passes and does not return.*
Psalm 78:38-39

My daughter, Faith, cleverly scheduled a doctor's appointment for my one- and four-year-old granddaughters' vaccines on a day she was working.

"Dad, can you take the girls for their shots?"

I love hanging out with my grands, so I immediately said, "Sure. I'd love to."

Then—after I hung up—I realized the implications. That realization burst full force as I held the one-year-old kicking and screaming—with sheer terror, looking me right in the eyes—as the nurse stuck her with two shots. Her older sister made a run for the door, knowing she was next to endure this humiliating torture. "No, Papaw!"

I scooped her up in my free hand and held her tight as both girls screaming bloody murder—obviously at the hands of their once-loving, protective papaw.

All the time, I was thinking, *Well played, Faith. Well played.*

Despite my attempts to explain to the girls that measles, mumps, rubella, diphtheria, tetanus, and pertussis are a thousand times worse than a pinprick, for the rest of the day I was *grandpa non grata*. And all the ice cream at Culver's could not convince them that Papaw really did love them, despite terrorizing and torturing them.

If you're a parent, you know that sickening feeling as you forcefully hold down your beloved child for shots, stitches, and other painful medical procedures. You feel like a terrible parent—and your child screams that you are, indeed, terrible. But you also know that your love for your child forces you to do things that now are painful, but will ensure a healthy future.

We feel like that child when a masked man knocks us out, slashes open our chests, and takes our money. But our lives have been saved by the *cardiologist*!

Now, if we just had that confidence in a good God when bad things happen to us.

In my favorite scene from *The Lion, the Witch and the Wardrobe*, Susan asks if the great lion, Aslan, is safe.

"'Safe?' said Mr. Beaver. . . . 'Who said anything about safe? 'Course he isn't safe. But he's good.'"[45]

God is not safe! Unfortunately, some church leaders have taught a declawed and domesticated "Kitty Cat of Judah." The *Lion* of Judah is not safe, but he is good. That's his character, and we need to trust God's character instead of earthly circumstances.

The Nature of God

The goodness of God was poured out on the cross—blood and water . . . and love—so our sins could be forgiven and we could have an eternal relationship with him.

After a lecture at the University of Chicago in 1962, a student asked the renowned theologian, Karl Barth, if he could summarize his whole life's work in theology in a sentence. Barth reportedly answered, "Jesus loves me this I know. For the Bible tells me so."[46]

If anyone grew up in a Christian home, that children's chorus is probably the most memorable. And if you attended Sunday school as a child, the very first verse you ever memorized was John 3:16: "For God so loved the world. . . ." Throughout the Bible, God's love for his creation has been proclaimed.

> Know therefore that the LORD your God, He is God, the faithful God, who keeps His covenant and His loving-kindness to a thousandth generation with those who love Him and keep His commandments . . . (Deuteronomy 7:9).

> How precious is your unfailing love, O God! All humanity finds shelter in the shadow of your wings (Psalm 36:7 NLT)

> "For the LORD your God is living among you. He is a mighty savior. He will take delight in you with gladness. With his love, he will calm all your fears. He will rejoice over you with joyful songs" (Zephaniah 3:17 NLT).

> For while we were still helpless, at the right time Christ died for the ungod-

> ly. For one will hardly die for a righteous man; though perhaps for the good man someone would dare even to die. But God demonstrates His own love toward us, in that while we were yet sinners, Christ died for us. Much more then, having now been justified by His blood, we shall be saved from the wrath of God through Him. For if while we were enemies we were reconciled to God through the death of His Son, much more, having been reconciled, we shall be saved by His life. And not only this, but we also exult in God through our Lord Jesus Christ, through whom we have now received the reconciliation (Romans 5:5-11).

We are unconditionally, inconceivably loved by God, even when we face questions, pain, and disappointments.

Therese of Lisieux writes:

> [We must remain] a little child before the good God. . . . It is recognizing one's nothingness, expecting everything from the good God, just as a little child expects everything from its father, it is not anxious, not trying to make one's fortune, . . . never being disheartened by one's faults, because children often fall, but they are too little to do themselves much harm.[47]

My friend, Lissa Halls Johnson, spoke to a writers' conference about the dishonesty of a lot of Christian writing and speaking.

> Instead of writing in a way that tells the truth of God's *full* character, we focus only on the pleasant aspects of God's character and behavior (grace, truth, kindness, love, mercy, etc), or the aspects which suit our purpose in convicting unbelievers (righteousness, judgment, eternal damnation).
>
> Why is this? Personally, I think it's that we don't know what to do with the whole truth about God. It's frightening, and so we're afraid of the truth.
>
> I think if we are to be truthful writers, we must face our fears about God and wrestle with them as Jacob did all night in the desert. [48]

I'm afraid our ideal of fatherhood comes from 1950s "sitcoms" rather than Scripture. In Jewish culture, the father had absolute authority, if you dishonored or spoke back to him, you found yourself under a pile of stones (Leviticus 20:9). Not exactly the wit, warmth, and whimsy of Andy Griffith.

According to the Talmud, an extra-biblical compilation of Jewish civil and ceremonial law, Jewish fathers were only required to teach their sons three things: to earn a living, to study scripture each day, and to swim.

That seems rather coldly practical. And yet, Brother Lawrence writes in his classic devotional:

> God knoweth best what is needful for us, and all that He does is for our good. If we knew how much He loves us, we should always be ready to receive equally and with indifference from His hand the sweet and the bitter. All would

please that came from Him. The sorest afflictions never appear intolerable, except when we see them in the wrong light. When we see them as dispensed by the hand of God, when we know that it is our loving Father who abases and distresses us, our sufferings will lose their bitterness and become even matter of consolation.

Let all our employment be to know God.

To me, God is like a no-nonsense, tough-love trainer who believes in me, wants what's best for me, but he's not going to go easy on me. "No discipline is enjoyable while it is happening—it's painful! But afterward there will be a peaceful harvest of right living for those who are trained in this way" (Hebrews 12:11).

The concept of trainer and trainee seems to be the way he works in my life. Paul uses the boxing metaphor in his writing: "All athletes are disciplined in their training. They do it to win a prize that will fade away, but we do it for an eternal prize. So I run with purpose in every step. I am not just shadowboxing" (1 Corinthians 9:25-26).

I don't always understand his training program, but I know his purpose is for my good. Our son, Paul, after graduating from college, held several jobs that—let's just say—were not exactly a match for his talents and passions. He writes:

> I have certainly had my fill of jobs that I didn't like. But I found that the Lord worked through them anyway. In many ways, the horrible jobs prepared me for this dream job.
>
> Don't count those types of jobs out. If I had not walked through the horrible ones, I wouldn't have been ready for this one. Don't miss the blessings the

> Lord has for you, just because you might have to ask, "Do you want fries with that?" The Lord could be saying, "I can only truly bless you if you are willing to do the hard, mundane and unfulfilling types of work."
>
> Some of his best work on me was done at those times. That's what he taught me and it was truly worth it.[49]

Our "dangerously creative" child has grown into a talented musician, actor, voice-over artist, and scriptwriter who now serves full time as creative director of children's ministries in a large church. I couldn't be prouder of him.

It can take time and a pattern of God's faithfulness, for us to truly trust that he has our best interests at heart. And then, that trust in his character gives us hope as troubles continue—and often escalate. Job proclaims, "'Though He slay me, I will hope in Him'" (13:15).

Our oldest grandson used to fear that Grandpa would push him too high in the swing or not "spot" him as he climbed playground equipment. But he learned to trust me and it wasn't long before he was shouting "Higher! Higher!" And fearlessly leaping from the monkey bars into my arms.

A. W. Tozer sums it up well: "My faith does not rest on God's promises. My faith rests upon God's character. Faith must rest in confidence upon the One who made the promises."[50] Amy Simpson further explains as she writes about changing worry into trust:

> Changing worry means changing what we believe about God and ourselves. If we don't believe God is any bigger or better than us, we have reason to fret. But if we believe He's all-powerful, trustworthy, righteous, and good, it

makes sense not to waste our lives in worry, but instead to believe and embrace what we know to be true about God and who we are as His children.[51]

Asaph could confidently write:

But He led forth His own people like sheep
And guided them in the wilderness like a flock;
He led them safely, so that they did not fear;
But the sea engulfed their enemies.
So He brought them to His holy land,
To this hill country which His right hand had gained.

So he shepherded them according to the integrity of his heart,
And guided them with his skillful hands.
Psalm 78:52-54, 72

13
There Is a Purpose

*With Your counsel You will guide me,
And afterward receive me to glory.
Whom have I in heaven but You?
And besides You, I desire nothing on earth.
My flesh and my heart may fail,
But God is the strength of my heart and my portion forever.*
Psalm 73:24-26

If you have children, nieces and nephews, or younger siblings, you know that a three-year-old's favorite word is *why*.

"Johnny, hold my hand while we cross the street."

"Why?"

"Because I don't want you to run out in front of a car."

"Why?"

"Because if a car hits you, you'll be hurt or killed."

"Why?"

"Because if it's a contest between a thirty-five-pound boy and an SUV, the three-ton vehicle is going to win every time."

"Why?"

"Because the laws of physics state that mass plus momentum equals—Just take my hand, Johnnie!"

And on it goes—right into adulthood!

The Book of Job is a book of why questions, but it doesn't end with answers. It ends with even more questions. Sixty-six to be exact—from God himself. Job 38-40 is the ultimate "pop quiz."

Geology: "Where were you when I laid the foundations of the earth? Who determined its measures, if you know? Or who stretched the line on it? Whereupon were its foundations fastened? Or who laid its cornerstone?"

Astrophysics: "Do you know the laws of the universe? Can you use them to regulate the earth? Where does light come from, and where does darkness go?"

Meteorology: "Does the rain have a father? Who gives birth to the dew? Who is the mother of the ice? Who gives birth to the frost from the heavens? For the water turns to ice as hard as rock, and the surface of the water freezes."

Zoology: "Have you watched as deer are born in the wild? Do you know how many months they carry their young? Are you aware of the time of their delivery?"

And, of course, theology: "Do you still want to argue with the Almighty? You are God's critic, but do you have the answers? Will you discredit my justice and condemn me just to prove you are right?"

Job is overwhelmed with this rapid-fire interrogation. "I am nothing—how could I ever find the answers? I will cover my mouth with my hand. I have said too much already. I have nothing more to say" (40:4-5).

But God moves on to the bonus round with another chapter of million-dollar questions (Job 41).

> Then Job answered the LORD and said,
> "I know that You can do all things,
> And that no purpose of Yours can be thwarted. 'Who is this that hides

> counsel without knowledge?' Therefore I have declared that which I did not understand, Things too wonderful for me, which I did not know." 'Hear, now, and I will speak; I will ask You, and You instruct me.' "I have heard of You by the hearing of the ear; But now my eye sees You; Therefore I retract, And I repent in dust and ashes" (42:1-6).

And though Job had no answers for any of the sixty-six questions, he still wins the grand prize!

> The LORD restored the fortunes of Job when he prayed for his friends, and the LORD increased all that Job had twofold. Then all his brothers and all his sisters and all who had known him before came to him, and they ate bread with him in his house; and they consoled him and comforted him for all the adversities that the LORD had brought on him. And each one gave him one piece of money, and each a ring of gold. The LORD blessed the latter *days* of Job more than his beginning . . . (42:10-12).

We may never know the answers to our greatest questions. Like Job, once I have had an encounter with God, I am brought to my knees with the realization, "I was talking about things I knew nothing about, things far too wonderful for me."

> "For My thoughts are not your thoughts, Nor are your ways My ways," declares the LORD (Isaiah 55:8).

> Oh, how great are God's riches and wisdom and knowledge! How impossible it is for us to understand his decisions and his ways!
>
> For who can know the Lord's thoughts? Who knows enough to give him advice? And who has given him so much that he needs to pay it back?
>
> For everything comes from him and exists by his power and is intended for his glory. All glory to him forever! Amen (Romans 11:33-36 NLT).

Thomas à Kempis writes:

> My friend, don't argue about the hidden workings of God that are beyond your comprehension. Do not ask, why is this person seemingly neglected and this person shown such great favor? Why is this person greatly afflicted and this one so highly exalted? These things are beyond human power of understanding. Divine judgments are beyond earthly reasoning, arguments, or explanations. So, when the enemy of our soul—or curious people—ask such questions, answer with the words of the psalmist: "O Lord, you are righteous, and your regulations are fair" (Psalm 119:137).
>
> Also answer: "The laws of the Lord are true; each one is fair" (Psalm

19:9). My judgments are to be feared, not to be disputed, because they are incomprehensible to human understanding.[52]

And like the popular game show, *Jeopardy*, the answers are in the form of a question.

What Can I Know?

I've worked up way too much spiritual perspiration trying to answer why my second-grade teacher committed suicide, why I was laid off from the perfect job in publishing—twice—or why bad things happen to such good people as you and me.

I have learned that while *why* is often a futile question, God is more than willing to answer other questions.

A. B. Simpson, author and founder of the Christian and Missionary Alliance, wrote:

> We often ask the question, "Why didn't God help me sooner?" It is not His order. He must first adjust us to the situation and cause us to learn our lesson from it. His promise is, I will be with him in trouble; I will deliver him, and honor him. He first must be with us in the trouble until we grow quiet. Then he will take us out of it. This will not come until we have stopped being restless and fretful about it and have become calm and trustful. Then he will say, "It is enough."
>
> God uses trouble to teach his children precious lessons. They are intended to educate us. When their good work is done, a glorious recompense will come to us through them. He does not regard them as difficulties but as

> opportunities. They have come to give God a greater interest in us and to show how he can deliver us from them. Without difficulties we cannot have a mercy worth praising God for. God is as deep, and long, and high as our little world of circumstances.[53]

God's Word backs up Simpson's challenge:

> But if any of you lacks wisdom, let him ask of God, who gives to all generously and without reproach, and it will be given to him. But he must ask in faith without any doubting, for the one who doubts is like the surf of the sea, driven and tossed by the wind. For that man ought not to expect that he will receive anything from the Lord, *being* a double-minded man, unstable in all his ways (James 1:5-8).

So, while I've struggled with hundreds—probably thousands—of questions about God's workings, I have grown in my knowledge of *who* he is. While agonizing about an estranged relationship, I burst into tears—for God. I had described to a friend my pain: "It feels like my heart has been cut out with a chainsaw, run over by a logging truck, and then fed through a wood chipper." If I was feeling this excruciating pain for one broken relationship, how was God feeling about billions of heartaches? It was one of the few times I actually felt I understood God.

I can also find the answer to . . .

How Can I Grow?

Remember the "purpose" to which "all things work together for good"? To "be conformed to the image of his son" (Romans 8:28).

> And the Lord—who is the Spirit—*makes us more and more like him* as we are changed into his glorious image (2 Corinthians 3:18b, *author's emphasis*).
>
> *Be imitators of God*, therefore, as dearly loved children and live a life of love, just as Christ loved us and gave himself up for us as a fragrant offering and sacrifice to God (Ephesians 5:1, *author's emphasis*).
>
> We have this treasure in earthen vessels, so that the surpassing greatness of the power will be of God and not from ourselves; we are afflicted in every way, but not crushed; perplexed, but not despairing; persecuted, but not forsaken; struck down, but not destroyed; always carrying about in the body the dying of Jesus, *so that the life of Jesus also may be manifested in our body* (2 Corinthians 4:7-10, *author's emphasis*).

There it is again: becoming conformed to the image of Christ. That's our purpose! Thomas à Kempis writes:

> Jesus has many lovers of his heavenly kingdom but few bearers of his cross. He has many seekers of comfort but few willing to face troubles and trial. He finds many companions at his table but few with him in fasting. Many desire to rejoice with him, but few are willing to undergo adversity for his sake. Many follow Jesus that they may

> eat of his bread, but few are willing to drink of the cup of his passion. Many are astonished at his miracles, but few follow after the shame of his cross. Many love Jesus so long as no troubles happen to them. Many praise him and bless him, so long as they receive comforts from him.
>
> But those who love Jesus for Jesus' sake—and not for the comforts he gives to them—praise him in all suffering and sorrow just as they do in the greatest blessings. And if he should never give them another blessing, they would nevertheless continue to always praise him and give him thanks.
> Oh, how powerful is the pure love of Jesus—unmixed with any material benefits or love of self![54]

One of the most meaningful compliments I've ever received was a typo—a God-inspired misspelling: "Thank you for your *wounderful* writing." Out of our woundedness comes something wonderful. Frederick William Robertson writes:

> The best things of life come out of wounding. Wheat is crushed before it becomes bread. Incense must be cast upon the fire before its odors are set free. The ground must be broken with the sharp plough before it is ready to receive the seed. It is the broken heart that pleases God. The sweetest joys in life are the fruits of sorrow. Human nature seems to need suffering to fit it for being a blessing to the world.[55]

A friend wrote on Facebook following a loveless marriage and painful divorce:

> It is amazing how God works in the midst of anger, frustration, hurt, and tears. It is amazing that through that pain, he continues to be steady and stable and, if you let him, he will make the process sweet through the pain. I have been clinging to the promise of "beauty from ashes" and trusting that there is a plan at work. Frankly, I have been overwhelmed to tears to see how he has been orchestrating my life. I have also been overwhelmed to tears to see how far I have come and how sturdy I've grown in my faith. I am so in awe of the love that Jesus pours into us if we choose to see by faith, completely trusting that, although we can not see into tomorrow, that in the end, God's got this and we will be okay. Wow! What a sweet, sweet thing that is.[56]

Author Elizabeth Kulber Ross, a leading expert on death, writes about how life's challenges make us better, more beautiful people.

> The most beautiful people we have known are those who have known defeat, known suffering, known struggle, known loss, and have found their way out of the depths.
> These persons have an appreciation, a sensitivity, and an understanding of life that fills them with compassion, gentleness, and a deep loving concern.
>
> Beautiful people do not just happen.[57]

And here's a curious thing about becoming holy people through the work of the Son and the power of the Spirit: The more righteous we become, the more wretched we realize we are. It goes back to my illustration of Adolph Hitler, Mother Teresa, and a holy God. The more we become like Jesus, the more we realize we how distant we are from Christ-likeness.

A second curious thing: We're even not aware that we're living a holy life. I wrote in my journal in April 2008:

> Still am amazed that someone would write on their [writers' conference] evaluation, "I can see Jesus in Jim." Have these dreadful past five years "worked together" according to that "purpose"? Am I finally starting to imitate Christ!

So, ask how can you grow through this difficult time. L. Thomas Holdcroft offers this encouraging insight:

> Christianity may not always offer supernatural deliverance from earth's problems, but it always offers supernatural use for them. It is likely that Peter, who was delivered from prison, learned less than Paul, who stayed there. [58]

And finally . . .

Who Can I Show?

Second Corinthians 1:3-6 has become one of my favorite passages in encouraging me while I'm going through terrible times:

> Praise be to the God and Father of our Lord Jesus Christ, the Father of com-

> passion and the God of all comfort, who comforts us in all our troubles, so that we can comfort those in any trouble with the comfort we ourselves have received from God. For just as the sufferings of Christ flow over into our lives, so also through Christ our comfort overflows. If we are distressed, it is for your comfort and salvation; if we are comforted, it is for your comfort, which produces in you patient endurance of the same sufferings we suffer (NLT).

The Greek word translated comfort is *paraklesis*. It is a calling near, summons for help; a prayer, a plea; exhortation, admonition, encouragement; consolation, comfort, solace, refreshment; or a persuasive speech, motivational talk, instruction. And it's feminine case. No one comforts like a mother.

We offer our best comfort to those experiencing what we have personally gone through. When best-selling author and mega-church pastor, Rick Warren, and his wife Kay lost their son to suicide, they immediately became qualified to minister to those who have dealt with mental illness and suicide.

Warren told ChristianPost.com:

> In the middle of all that intense pain, Kay and I have felt the favor of God because of your prayers, and we intend to spend the rest of our lives comforting others with the comfort we ourselves have been given by God.
>
> For 27 years I prayed every day of my life for God to heal my son's mental illness. . . . It didn't make sense why this prayer wasn't being answered.

> When you go through a difficult time, you automatically start to try and find an answer. But explanations never comfort. You don't need explanations; you need the presence of God.[59]

Men and women who have never faced a serious illness, never had an argument with their other half, never owed a cent of debt, always had well-behaved children, worked at a perfect job with a perfect boss, and retired to Hawaii with a huge pension should not write books. They would never sell, because they have nothing to offer the rest of us.

I wrote about this concept in my book *Squeezing Good Out of Bad*:

> I made myself a list of things for which I can now comfort others that I had absolutely no experience with fresh out of the ministerial classroom with an ordination certificate in hand and pat answers on my lips. In alphabetical order they are listed below:
>
> - Audit by the IRS
> - Building programs
> - Cancer
> - Depression
> - Eye disease (I'm legally blind in my left eye)
> - Financial pressures
> - Gas prices
> - Harassing phone calls
> - India
> - Jury duty
> - Kidney stone

- Living in a girls' dorm for six years (Let the record show, my wife was RD)
- Marital strife
- Nose hair
- Obesity
- Parsonage fire caused by my cooking
- Quotes taken out of context
- Robbery of the parsonage
- Slander by an insubordinate subordinate
- Traveling twelve hours in a van full of junior-high boys—who had just eaten at Taco Bell!
- Unanswered prayer
- Visiting a parishioner in the closed section of a mental hospital and then, before leaving, having to prove I wasn't a patient
- Worship wars (hymns v. choruses, hymnals v. video, etc.)
- X-rated temptations
- Youth over-nighters
- Zits

[God] has used physical pain to move me past annoyance with old people's complaints ("Come on, Gramps, stop obsessing about your colon!"), to a real empathy for anyone in pain. Yep, God even works together for good stubborn kidney stones, double-hernia surgery, and central serous retinopathy (a

$200-an-hour ophthalmologist's term for looking at life just a bit differently than normal people). Now, I even get false labor pains whenever I visit the maternity ward.

But more than physical pain, God has used emotional pain to make me a more loving, understanding person. When I started out in youth work during the Polyester Era, my counseling philosophy was simply, "Get over it!"

Now that I'm diagnosed with clinical depression [plus ADD, OCD and a touch of Autism], I have much more empathy for people whom I used to think didn't have any willpower or control over their thinking processes. "Just quit your stinkin' thinkin'!" I might as well tell a diabetic, "You don't need insulin, just a better attitude toward your blood-sugar levels!"

I even have a better understanding of how God feels after an estranged relationship.

I don't credit—or blame—God for any of this pain or planned obsolescence. But I do praise him that he has used times of physical, mental, and emotional pain to chip away at my sharp edges. And it has allowed me to provide real comfort for others losing their looks, their jobs, or their health.

Let me give you an update on the first three examples of unanswered prayer, unfulfilled promises, and unpunished evil:

Unanswered prayer

I began this book with the story of Dave, who apparently was miraculously healed of pancreatic cancer—one of the worst kinds—after prayer and anointing by his church only to find out the "healing" was a cruel mis-diagnosis. Then as the church prayed for the surgery, an artery tore, and Dave bled to death even as Facebook pleas for prayer went out.

Here's how his wife, Teresa, describes the tragic events:

> When we found out that in fact the tumor on Dave's pancreas was not healed but still there, I felt like God was testing my faith in him. Dave was in shock and not talking much about it. We both still felt like God would take care of it.
>
> After all the praying during this time and the nonstop praying during the ten-hour surgery, all seemed to be going well. The cancer had not spread!
>
> Then, one of the doctors came out and told us that when they were removing the tumor, they discovered it was intertwined around one of the arteries, and when they removed the tumor, the artery tore and Dave was bleeding out. They said he had already had one heart attack from all the blood loss, and wanted to know what I wanted to do. All I could think of was for them to do whatever they had to do to save him. I couldn't lose him now. Surely, God wouldn't do that. They told me there was one other thing they could try,

but they didn't think he would make it through the night. I told them to try, because I was still counting on God to save him for me.

About twenty minutes later the doctors came out and said he was gone!

At that time, I thought God was punishing me for my past mistakes. I was still going to church and hoping God would answer my questions. Then I started going to one of our church's small groups. All the people there were so caring and understanding. They helped me to put my faith back in God's promises and to know God that does not punish. He always there for us no matter what.

Then just three years later, I was diagnosed with breast cancer, but God assured me he was there for me, and all would be okay. I'm now cancer-free.

I believe God has a reason for everything. We may not always know the answer at the time. Recently, my son-in- law was diagnosed with the same cancer and we lost him after much pain and suffering.

God is great no matter what the outcome. All my faith is still in him.[60]

Teresa has proven to be a powerful witness to a life submitted to God's will in the death of her husband, her own cancer battle, and recently the death of her son-in-law—who is also the pastor's brother. She radiates a joy that only comes in knowing the love of God.

The church has also kept the faith and has doubled in size and faith which is based on God's character, not circumstances. It's not how I would have planned it, but I guess that's why God doesn't invite me to his committee meetings.

Unfulfilled promises

I began this book with my confession that Malachi 3:10-11's promise—if you tithe, you will be will receive "over-flowing" blessings—hadn't seemed to be fulfilled in my life.

I believed—and still do—that tithing is the biblical method for financing God's work and caring for "the least of these." Jesus teaches in Matthew 23:23:

> "What sorrow awaits you teachers of religious law and you Pharisees. Hypocrites! For you are careful to tithe even the tiniest income from your herb gardens, but you ignore the more important aspects of the law—justice, mercy, and faith. *You should tithe*, yes, but do not neglect the more important things (NLT, *author's emphasis*).

Jesus did not abolish tithing. Instead, he expanded the manner and motivation for giving:

> "Don't store up treasures here on earth, where moths eat them and rust destroys them, and where thieves break in and steal. Store your treasures in heaven, where moths and rust cannot destroy, and thieves do not break in and steal. Wherever your treasure is, there the desires of your heart will also be" (Luke 6:19-20 NLT).

Giving is no longer about simply—and legalistically—giving one-tenth of our income. Tithing also includes our time and talents to fulfill "the more important aspects of the law—justice, mercy, and faith." The Old Testament stresses the letter of the law; the New Testament the spirit of the law.

And finally, tithing does produce a "blessing." The Hebrew word for blessing is Barakah. It can mean blessing; the praise of God; a gift, a present; a peace treaty; liberality. It's used sixty-nine times in the Old Testament, but rarely in reference to financial blessings. Most of the time it denotes godly rewards rather than earthly riches.

So, here are some "answers" I've come to after years of struggling financially and spiritually.

First, Jesus taught "'Blessed are you who are poor, for yours is the kingdom of God'" (Luke 6:20, author's emphasis). Unlike his Sermon on the Mount, where he uses "poor in spirit," the Sermon on the Plain speaks of literal poverty. Jesus' teachings turn the world's values upside down. So, there have been times I felt very blessed!

Second, I may not have had a large bank account or a retirement fund for most of my life, but I have been abundantly Barakah-ed!

I have been blessed with godly parents, wife, adult children, and adorable grandchildren. I've been blessed to live longer than my maternal grandfather, despite a cancer scare. (Cancer-free since 2008!)

God has given me the privilege to share at camps, churches, colleges, and conferences throughout the United States and overseas, as well as through books and articles. I've been blessed to meet wonderful authors, musicians, and national religious leaders, many of whom have become good friends.

Plus—materially—I have been Barakah-ed to have never slept on the street, never missed a meal, always had a closet filled with clothes, and always had a vehicle. (At the time, my 2004 Taurus had 220,000 miles, but it still ran and had been purchased with cash.)

Unfortunately, we always seemed to have "just enough, just in time." The only thing "overflowing" was our credit card bill envelopes.

So, when I originally wrote this section, I was careful not to imply that God promised to bless us financially. But, in all honesty, Malachi describes physical and financial rewards:

> "Your crops will be abundant, for I will guard them from insects and disease. Your grapes will not fall from the vine before they are ripe," says the LORD of Heaven's Armies" (3:11).

I was trying to give God some wiggle room if readers felt he was failing the test financially for them as well. But God does not need my "spin."

After twenty years of just getting by, I received an inheritance which was "infinitely more than we might ask or think" (Ephesians 3:20). At this point, our mortgage, second mortgage, and credit card balances are paid off. We've been able to give significant donations to our favorite Christian charities. And we now have enough invested to give us earthly security if this writing and speaking thing doesn't work out.

Recently, my friend Gary caught me in the hall at church and simply said, "I told you so."

"Told me what?"

"Just think about it," he answered with a big grin.

A few years earlier, in our men's Bible study, I confessed that the old platitude, "You can't out give God," was simply not true in my life. Gary disagreed—and he was right! It took nearly twenty years, but I now know that God does keep his promises—even Malachi 3:10! Not on our schedule, but he keeps every single promise in his time. (If I had received the money much earlier, I probably would have blown through it with matching new Mustangs, a time-share in Maui, and more stuff I really don't need.)

So, if you're going through a rough time financially, be encouraged.

- Thank him for the faith development and spiritual growth he is providing as you go through this difficult and painful time of want—and it is difficult and painful.
- Concentrate on the spiritual riches he is pouring out on you in reward for your white-knuckled obedience. Make a list.
- Learn the lessons he has for you during this time of discipline and testing.

- And always remember all the time, he always keeps his promises—in his time.

Unpunished evil

As this book began, I used Islamic terrorism as an example of unpunished evil. But God is working something truly good through something totally evil. I received this email from a purposely-unidentified worker in the Middle East.

> I was recently in Beirut sitting in a room with twenty-one Syrian Kurdish refugee women, most of whom had become followers of Jesus only because of ISIS, essentially. Only because of ISIS, they fled their homes and were then ministered to by Christians in Beirut. It was truly an amazing miracle. I was also in a few other Muslim majority countries recently (I can't say which ones, for security reasons) and was dialoguing with church leaders. One leader said, "We are thankful for ISIS because they are doing the work for us! People are leaving Islam!" All of our jaws dropped, at first almost in disgust, but then mostly in praise to God about how he is using these horrifying, terrifying, and apocalyptic events to make himself known and to bring people to the Truth. So, keep up the prayer. That is the *number one* message that I've gotten from people in the region. This is happening and can only continue happening through prayer. I asked the question essentially,

"What can we in the West do?" *Everyone* said "Pray, pray, pray."[61]

A headline from the *Voice of the Martyrs* magazine concurs: "ISIS Pushing Muslims Toward Christ."

> As the self-proclaimed Islamic State (ISIS) continues to advance across Iraq and Syria, it not only persecutes Christians, but also pushes Muslims toward Christ. Its efforts to create a "pure" Islamic nation are causing a growing number of Muslims to examine their faith more closely and more critically. "There are a lot of people turning from Islam," said Ibrahim Al-Jamil, a pastor in northern Iraq. "Jesus has a big net and ISIS is pushing people toward this net."
>
> What we are seeing now is like the tip of the iceberg. Ibrahim said he also sees evidence on social media and elsewhere on the Internet that Muslims are leaving Islam. He said, "They are repulsed by what ISIS is doing and increasingly disagree with Islam's teachings."
>
> ISIS is making people, especially Muslims, think about their faith and question the faith they were born in and don't understand," he said.[62]

What an amazing modern-day example of the truth that Joseph proclaimed to his brothers who beat him and sold him into slavery: "You intended to harm me, but God intended it all for good" (Genesis 50:20 NLT).

I think Joseph would have agreed with Douglas Adams who observes, "I may not have gone where I intended to go, but I think I have ended up where I needed to be.[63]"

Those two statements pretty much sum up this book, as does this eulogy I wrote for one of my favorite questioners, who died much too young after a lifetime of medical misadventures:

In Memory of Gerry Peters

Gerry Peters finally has all her questions answered.

After Lois led her to Christ and she began attending our church, at least once a week, I'd get a call from Gerry. With her Brooklyn directness, she would skip the phone formalities and launch right in with a question:

"When did Jesus know he was God? Did he know it as a little boy? Or did he only know after God his Father announced it at his baptism?

"Why did God allow freewill? Why did he allow evil? How can he be in control and still let people do such hateful things?"

"If we have a sin that we keep doing and we come to God for forgiveness each time, does he know we keep doing it, or has he totally forgotten it? And how can someone who is all-knowing, *not* know something?"

My response was always, "Oh, hi, Gerry. That's a great question. I'll have to think about that and get back with you."

Gerry could ask the most profound questions because of her profound love for Christ. And every conversation ended with "I just love him so much."

After her heart failure and subsequent brain damage, her questions became more childlike, but still equally profound.

"Why did God make me stay here? I just want to go to heaven and be with Jesus. I just love him so much."

"Why did God allow my brother to be murdered? Why my brother and not me. I just want to go to heaven and be with Jesus. I just love him so much."

"Why did God make me stay here. I just want to go to heaven . . ."

And my reply was always, "Oh, hi, Gerry. That's a great question. I'll have to think about that and get back with you."
So, thanks, Gerry, for all your profound and thought-provoking questions. They stretched my thinking. And most of all, thank you for your love for Christ, your pastors, and people of the church.

Even in heaven, I'm sure she's still asking questions. Today, however,

Jesus himself replies, "That's a great question." But he doesn't have to think about it. He doesn't have to say, "I'll get back with you."

Jesus answers all her questions. Every one of them. Patiently. Perfectly. Profoundly.

And I'm sure she ends each conversation with her Lord by saying, "I just love you so much."

Thanks for joining me in examining the evidence and listening to eyewitnesses in the mysterious case of unanswered prayer, unfulfilled promises, and unpunished evil. I hope it has encouraged you as it has encouraged me. Unlike a TV trial, all the questions are not answered and every detail is not tied up in a neat bow. So, if you'd like to continue the "deliberation," I'd love for you to comment at jameswatkins.com/asaph/. And if you found it helpful, please tell your family and friends, social media followers, and be sure to write an online review. Thanks.

Hopefully, you and I have been assured that even though life is hard, God is good, and he is redeeming his purpose in every hard place. And for that, we can give thanks.

David gave to Asaph and his fellow Levites this song of thanksgiving to the Lord:

Give thanks to the Lord and proclaim his greatness.
Let the whole world know what he has done.
Sing to him; yes, sing his praises.
Tell everyone about his wonderful deeds.
Exult in his holy name;
rejoice, you who worship the Lord.
Search for the Lord and for his strength;
continually seek him.
Remember the wonders he has performed,
his miracles, and the rulings he has given,

you children of his servant Israel,
you descendants of Jacob, his chosen ones.
He is the LORD our God.
His justice is seen throughout the land.
Remember his covenant forever—
the commitment he made to a thousand generations.

Give thanks to the LORD, for he is good!
His faithful love endures forever.
Cry out, "Save us, O God of our salvation!
Gather and rescue us from among the nations,
so we can thank your holy name
and rejoice and praise you."
Praise the LORD, the God of Israel,
who lives from everlasting to everlasting!
And all the people shouted "Amen!" and praised the LORD.

1 Chronicles 16:7-15, 34-36 NLT

About the Author

Jim Watkins is an award-winning author of more than twenty books and more than two thousand articles, who has spoken across the United States and overseas. He has served as an editor and editorial director at Wesleyan Publishing House, an editor with the American Bible Society, taught writing at Taylor University for fifteen years, and has guest-lectured at Liberty, Regent and other universities. He is currently writing and speaking full-time as well as editing for ACW Press and other clients. His most important roles, however, are being a child of God, husband, dad and "papaw."

Other Books by James N. Watkins

The Imitation of Christ
Classic Devotions in Today's Language

Squeezing Good Out of Bad
Top Ten Ways to Deal with Life's Lemons

Jesus
His Life and Lessons

Visit jameswatkins.com for book excerpts as well as columns and cartoons with "Hope & Humor"

(Endnotes)

1. (Romans 11:25; 1 Corinthians 2:7; Ephesians 5:32; 1 Timothy 3:9, 16).
2. https://www.goodreads.com/quotes/505827-discipleship-is-not-limited-to-what-you-can-comprehend--it-must
3. http://forum.thefreedictionary.com/postst145708_A-God-that-can-be-understood-is-no-God--Who-can-explain-the-Infinite-in-words-.aspx
4. William Cowper, *The Works of William Cowper: The life of William Cowper. Letters, 1765-1783*, Forgotten Books, 2017. p 150
5. David Brainerd and Jonathan Edwards, The Life of David Brainerd:Chiefly extracted from his Diary, Baker Book House, 1978. p 135.
6. Jonathan Edwards, et.al. The Works of Jonathan Edwards: The life of David Brainerd, Yale University Press, 1985. P 132
7. Ibid
8. C.S. Lewis, Letters to an American Lady, Eerdmans: Reissue Edition, 2014. P 95
9. September 21, 2017 Facebook https://www.facebook.com/AnnVoskamp/posts/1735113826500784
10. Used by permission.
11. The Lord is addressed as father in Deuteronomy 32:6; 1 Chronicles 29:10; Psalm 103:13; Proverbs 3:12; Isaiah 64:8, 16; Jeremiah 3:19; and Malachi 1:6, 2:10.
12. As quoted from A.W. Tozer *Tozer on Leadership* at https://www.biblegateway.com/devotionals/tozer-on-leadership/2015/04/17
13. https://www.mindbloom.com/apps/inspiration/detail/quote/7087bf1b-986b-4f3a-96f3-2df60621589d/
14. http://www.hopkinsmedicine.org/health/healthy_aging/healthy_connections/forgiveness-your-health-depends-on-it

15 James Watkins, *Squeezing Good Out of Bad* (Raleigh. Lighthouse Publishing of the Carolinas, 2013)

16 Let me throw this insight in for free. No extra charge. God loves "bookends." The Bible begins in a garden in Genesis and ends in a garden in Revelation. The ritual of Communion is comprised of Christ coming in flesh (bread) and dying for our sins (the wine)—tying together Christmas and Easter. Jesus is called the Alpha and Omega, the beginning and ending letters of the Greek alphabet. "In the beginning" there is no sun and in the last chapter there is no need for the sun. So, Jesus follows this pattern in his model prayer. And now back to our regularly-scheduled program . . .

17 Used by permission.

18 Used by permission.

19 H. Bonar, Answers-Streams in the Desert, July 10. Public Domain.

20 Mrs. Charles Cowan, *Streams in the Desert*, August 10. Public Domain.

21 Used by Permission.

22 Dallas Willard, *Living a Transformed Life Adequate to Our Calling*. *http://www.dwillard.org/articles/artview.asp?artID=119*

23 Thomas à Kempis, *The Imitation of Christ*, Book 3 Chapter 39. Public Domain.

24 Used by permission

25 Used by permission

26 Used by permission

27 George Matheson, Voices of the Spirit, Forgotten Books, 2017, p 184

28 C.S. Lewis, A Grief Observed (San Francisco: Harper San Francisco, 1996), pp. 5-7.

29 C.S. Lewis, *Words to Live By: A Guide for the Merely Christian*, Harper Collins, 2007, p 109.

30 Michelle Steele, *The Guilt the Shame and the Blood*, Amazon Digital Services LLC, 2012.

31   http://abcnews.go.com/US/indiana-pastor-speaks-heartbreak-pregnant-wifes-murder/story?id=35251892

32   http://people.com/crime/davey-blackburn-i-chose-the-route-of-forgiveness-grace-and-hope/

33   https://www.christianpost.com/news/amanda-blackburn-pastor-wife-killed-love-letter-jesus-151472/

34   https://www.christianpost.com/news/pastor-davey-blackburn-confused-about-pregnant-wifes-murder-150360/

35   Used by permission/.

36   Used by permission.

37   As quoted at http://www1.cbn.com/books/saving-a-serial-killer

38   https://www.goodreads.com/quotes/34482-life-is-difficult-this-is-a-great-truth-one-of

39   https://www.desiringgod.org/messages/to-live-upon-god-that-is-invisible

40   https://www.goodreads.com/quotes/1335487-we-re-easter-people-living-in-a-good-friday-world

41   Used by permission.

42   Used by permission.

43   Beverly Rose, So Close, I Can Feel God's Breath, Tyndale House Publishers, Salt River, 2006. P 127

44   Used by permission.

45   C. S. Lewis, The Lion, The Witch, and The Wardrobe, Chronicles of Narnia (Book 2), Zondervan; Reprint edition, 2009.

46   As quoted at http://www.patheos.com/blogs/rogereolson/2013/01/did-karl-barth-really-say-jesus-loves-me-this-i-know/

47   as quoted in Brandon Manning, *Abba's Child*, NavPress, 2015. p 69

48   Used by permission.

49   Used by permission.

50   A. W. Tozer, *Fiery Faith: Ignite Your Passion for God,* Wingspread, 2012.

51   https://thecounselingmoment.wordpress.com/tag/lie-based-thinking/

52   Kempis, (Book 3 Chapter 58).

53   http://www.cmalliance.org/devotions/simpson?mmdd=0926

54   Kempis (Book 2 Chapter 11).

55   Streams in the Desert, August 15. Public Domain

56   Used by permission.

57   http://www.ekrfoundation.org/quotes/

58   http://christiansquoting-dailyquotes.blogspot.com/2011/12/let-it-be-settled-principle-in-our.html
https://pathoflife.wordpress.com/author/pathoflife/page/80/

59   https://www.christianpost.com/news/rick-kay-warren-give-message-of-hope-during-first-sermon-back-since-sons-death-101020/

60   Used by permission

61   Used by permission.

62   https://www.vomcanada.com/static/nl-mar16.pdf

63   https://www.goodreads.com/quotes/3278-i-may-not-have-gone-where-i-intended-to-go

Made in the USA
Middletown, DE
08 January 2024